WHEAT- AND GLUTEN-FREE
HOME COOKING

DELICIOUS AND NUTRITIOUS RECIPES FOR THE WHOLE FAMILY

LOLA WORKMAN

APPLE

First published in the UK in 2006 by
Apple Press
Sheridan House
114 Western Rd
Hove
East Sussex BN3 1DD
www.apple-press.com

Author: Lola Workman
Publisher: Richard Carroll
Creative Director: Aisling Gallagher
Cover Design: Aisling Gallagher
Text Design: Design Corp
Production Manager: Anthony Carroll
Food Photography: Greg Elms, Jacek of Ad Libitum studios
Food Stylist: Sara Backhouse
Props: The Works, 275 Burwood Rd, Hawthorn, Victoria 3122, Tel: (03) 9810 6600
Recipe Development: Lola Workman
Proofreader: Fiona Brodribb, LoftCom

ISBN-10: 1 84543 170 7
ISBN-13: 978 1 84543 170 9

Printed in China by Max Production Printing Ltd.

CONTENTS

Letter from Lola

In this book I have finally achieved success with gluten-free pasta and extended my range of recipes to include a few main courses where wheat flour is commonly used. Most main courses do not or need not contain gluten, but some folk have difficulty converting their favourites. If you do need help remember I am just a letter, email or fax away, wherever you are. Most of the recipes are new, apart from the dozen or so favourites that are constantly used in gluten-free cookery classes; as *Wheat- and Gluten-Free Home Cooking* is now used as a teaching manual, these recipes such as crumpets, potato bread and my basic pastry have to stay.

Attention is drawn to the fact that my training is commercial cookery, and that medical details are not taught or discussed in this book, apart from recognition of the request of a gluten-free diet. I am not a dietitian trying to guess recipes by substituting gluten-free flour for wheat flour hoping that it will work; I am a trained cook who wishes to pass on the methods that I have found successful in this difficult subject. The methods are my own, adapted from my commercial training, research and experience gained over years of teaching cookery to adults and working with food intolerance and allergy sufferers. These methods have proved successful and easy to master even for inexperienced cooks.

My first published book *Lola's Wheat-Free World*, written for my allergy cookery classes, has now been used since 1996 by sufferers of coeliac disease and other intolerance conditions. My books come with ongoing recipe support by mail, fax and email to purchasers. Many letters of thanks are received each week from users of my recipes worldwide, who were not able to achieve success in their gluten-free cookery using other publications. Many have also complimented the detailed lesson-style format. Every recipe has been tested and baked many times over to achieve success without the use of xanthan or other chemical gums, the reason the book is used as a reference manual and recommended by medical practitioners throughout Australia.

This book is recognised by the National Coeliac Society of Australia.

Importance of Gluten in Cookery

GLUTEN

Gluten is a protein found in wheat, oats, barley, rye triticale and spelt. When mixed with liquid this element produces an elastic framework which stretches to contain the expanding gases during rising. The gluten content of flour holds their breads together preventing crumbling. Successful results in gluten-free cookery is dependent on a replacement for the missing gluten such as guar gum, xanthan gum, psyllium or gelatine, or eggs. While nothing can produce exactly the same results, products prepared in the correct manner will produce excellent results.

SWEETENERS IN COOKERY

Sucrose (table sugar) has many functions in food other than providing sweetness, so that caution is needed when sugar is omitted from a recipe. In small amounts, sugar is required to help yeast in fermenting, although in large amounts such as the amount used in buns, the sugar tenderises the dough but slows the rising process. In recipes such as pikelets, sugar helps to produce a golden brown colour. In cookie recipes a completely different result can occur by altering the type of sugar used. Doubling the quantity of sugar will create a toffee-like cookie that will spread in the oven.

Brown sugar will give you a softer result such as gingerbread.

Syrup and Treacle will produce toffee-like results as well as dark-coloured cookies.

Honey has a distinctive flavour and will produce a soft result that burns easily.

Fructose (fruit sugar) is nearly twice as sweet as sucrose and more expensive. It produces a moist darker result when baked.

Artificial sweeteners if used in cookery must be used strictly to manufacturers' instructions.

SALT

Salt is used to enhance the flavour in breads. In yeast dough, salt slows yeast fermentation, so reducing the salt causes the bread to rise too quickly, adversely affecting the flavour and shape of the bread, causing holes under the crust.

LEAVENING AGENTS

Bicarbonate of soda, also known as baking soda, produces a gas when mixed with an acidic substance such as vinegar, lemon juice or molasses for use in making damper, scones or some quick breads. If using vinegar in gluten-free cookery, wine vinegar can be used instead of malt vinegar.

BAKING POWDER

Baking powder is a mixture of baking soda and tartaric acid or other acid in the correct proportions to produce a gas. To evenly distribute the leavening ingredient, a filler is used in baking powders and it is this filler that can contain gluten, such as wheat starch. Be very careful to read the label of the baking powder you are using.

FATS

Fats are used in baking to add moisture and to add to the flavour of the product. A small amount of fat used in yeast dough will enable it to stretch and assist the rising. Oil gives a better result generally in gluten-free cookery, although butter is necessary for shortbread.

Collecting Utensils and Tins

Successful gluten-free cookery is dependent on one basic rule; commercial cooks weigh everything for consistent results. Expensive utensils are not necessary but a good electric mixer is very useful and I find a waffle iron invaluable. Keep your eyes open for bargains of heavy steel tins and interesting shapes such as teddy bear tins for children's lunch buns.

A paint scraper is useful for lifting pastry for tiny pie lids. Sheets of clear plastic will help you handle my warm gluten-free pastry.

Always weigh your dry ingredients; cup measurements will not give you consistent results with gluten-free flour. Cup measures are good for liquids; metric cups are used in this book. Level metric spoon measurements are important. The Australian tablespoon measures 20g used throughout this book.

The imported saddle tin below is made from heavy steel; it is used for the orange and poppy seed log as well as potato bread. Aluminium and some alloys do not cook gluten-free mixtures well, so always use steel tins. Aluminium will cook the edge of the cake well before the centre, giving a dry result. Steel cooks evenly. If the tins are coated, do not use cooking sprays for greasing as they form a film that will destroy the coating and cause your cake to stick. Margarine or butter is best for greasing tins.

Ingredient Substitutes

DAIRY PRODUCTS
Milk powder in my recipes can be replaced by extra gluten-free flour or arrowroot. Milk-free margarines are widely available and may be used.

CHICKPEA FLOUR
Often called besan, channa dahl, gram or bean flour, chickpea flour can be exchanged for Amaranth flour or other legume flours. Beware of soya bean flour, as many people are intolerant to soy products. Yellow pea flour is a cheaper flour that is sometimes bitter. Do not keep chickpea flour in an airtight container as it will quickly become rancid.

COCOA
Carob can be used instead of cocoa.

COCONUT
May be replaced with baby rice cereal and coconut essence.

CORN PRODUCTS
Corn can be avoided if my bread and pastry flour (page 11) is used throughout the book and the few recipes such as cornbreads are avoided. This flour can replace the all-purpose flour in all recipes.

DRIED FRUITS
Natural dried fruits that are unsulphured are available from health food shops. An electric dehydrator is a valuable appliance if you can't find unsulphured dried fruit.

EGGS
There are many egg replacements on the market worldwide. I have used several of them quite successfully but find that about double the recommended amount and at least double the amount of warm water is required for a good result; also warm water is better than cold for mixing. Egg white, either dried or fresh, can be substituted by the addition of 1 teaspoon amaranth cereal for each egg. In cake mixtures it is necessary to replace moisture lost by excluding the yolks. The amaranth cereal may be added to the flour. This is not necessary with egg replacer that includes gum.

BREAD IMPROVER
My gluten-free bread improver or dried egg white may be used to replace whole eggs if egg white is permitted. It is also useful to replace eggs in your own pre-mixes.

GELATINE/GELATIN
May be replaced by agar-agar products.

SUGAR
Sugar when used to 'feed' yeast in this book (eg. 1 teaspoonful), should not be substituted by artificial sweeteners. If the sugar is used as a sweetening agent (eg. over apples in a bun recipe), then cooking sweeteners may be used as replacement. Baby rice cereal is a good replacement for the added bulk of sugar if the mixture is too thin.

SEEDS
May be replaced by other garnishes such as coarse salt bacon or pepper.

VINEGAR
Wine vinegar may be replaced with cider or rice vinegar.

AMARANTH FLOUR AND CEREAL
This nutritious grain is now grown in Australia and milled to a flour. It is also produced as a breakfast cereal that can be used to replace psyllium in my recipes. The flour can be used to replace up to half the besan or chickpea flour in my blends.

Lola's Sauce Blocks

I created these blocks years ago for my cookery classes to simplify sauce making. They have proved invaluable as a replacement for milk in producing a basic dairy-free sauce that has many uses. This sauce is used as a base for producing your own preservative-free baby food and to prevent quiche curdling in a hot oven or to make a creamy fresh mushroom soup that is dairy-free. Once you have tried them you will never be without them in your freezer.

200g LOLA'S BREAD AND PASTRY FLOUR (page 11)
200g DAIRY-FREE MARGARINE

Melt the margarine in a saucepan over a low heat. Using a wooden spoon, stir in the flour.

Continue stirring and cook for about 3 minutes or until the mixture slides in the saucepan.

Pour the mixture into a 12–14 cup iceblock tray and refrigerate or freeze until required.

USING SAUCE BLOCKS

One block in 1 cup of boiling water or stock makes a thin sauce.
Two blocks makes a thick sauce as used for custard.

Dairy-Free Quiche: To the basic thin sauce whisk in 2 eggs for each cup of sauce; pour over the filling for your quiche. Bake immediately or freeze the raw quiche and bake later directly from the freezer. Great for mini quiche.

Masking Sauce: Season 1 cup of thin sauce for cauliflower or pasta-masking sauce.

Moussaka: Add 2 eggs to the thin sauce and pour over the meat and vegetables before baking.

Gravy: Heat two blocks with the juices in the baking tray after roasting to make a delicious gravy.

Mushroom or Green Asparagus Soup: Sauté fresh mushrooms and add to the thin sauce then blend in a can of green asparagus and juice.

Boutique Soups: Blend in watercress or green lettuce to the thin sauce and flavour with lemon or lime.

Pie Fillings: Use two blocks to thicken fillings such as mince or berries for pies.

Toast Topping: Tomatoes, bacon and onions thickened with one block.

Baby Food: Add chopped vegetables, fruit or meat to thin sauce; freeze in small containers.

Dairy-Free Custard: Whisk in 1 egg, sweeten and flavour as desired and cook for 1 minute.

Casseroles or Stew: Toss 1 or 2 blocks into the bubbling stew and stir until thickened.

Pumpkin Soup: One or 2 blocks will 'slake' your soup, suspending the vegetable evenly through the soup; just add them to the finished soup for a creamy result without cholesterol.

Nutritional Value of Chickpeas

One of the world's most ancient crops, chickpeas take their name from the beak-like shape that is prominent on the round body of the pea. They grow directly from the stem of the plant with a few pods on each branch, and only about two peas to a pod. The plant is insect resistant, thus eliminating the need for spraying with chemicals. Chickpeas are a hardy dry land crop that has been grown in quantity in many countries over the last twenty-five years. The majority of the peas grown in Australia are exported to Italy and India where they form a large part of the staple diet.

Two different strains of chickpeas are grown in Australia. Desi has a chocolate brown skin and is most commonly ground into flour which is characterised by tiny brown specks of skin. This flour is usually a cheaper chickpea flour than the golden-coloured flour blended from the larger kubuli pea. Either flour is called besan flour in Australia, although the flours are known by many other names throughout the world. The specks of skin impart an earthy taste to the flour. The golden-coloured flour has the better flavour for baking and blending into an all-purpose flour for gluten-free cookery.

Chickpeas are called garbanzo beans in America and flour from the peas is called dhal flour or channa dahl flour in India. In England and most of Europe it is known as gram flour. The smaller peas are often used as split peas for soups. These legumes are very high in protein, a wonderful fibre source and contain most vitamins and minerals. According to nutritionists, they contain a little fat of the 'right kind' and lots of those vital elements called anti-oxidants. They are a complex carbohydrate, meaning that the body takes a long time to break down their nutritional content, so they provide energy over a long period, a great help for diabetics, making very little demand on insulin.

Depending on the growing area and type of pea, moisture levels can vary but generally they provide a high level of moisture to baked goods where gluten cannot be used and are a blessing to coeliac and wheat-intolerance sufferers who cannot tolerate or do not like the strong taste of soy flour.

Intolerance to chickpeas is rare but caution is advised when introducing any new element to the diet.

Lola's Flour Blends

Formulation of these recipes came as a result of my cookery classes for food intolerance for those who cannot tolerate wheat or gluten in their diets. I have avoided using soya bean flour as many people are intolerant to it and children particularly don't like the strong taste.

There are many other gluten-free flour blends available but I have tested all that are available in Australia and found that they give a dry crumbly result unless a large amount of xanthan or guar gum is used. Nutrition should be considered when you are selecting a gluten-free replacement for wheat flour as simple mixes of rice and cornflour do not provide enough nutrition to replace wheat, particularly for children. Read the page on chickpeas and their nutrition.

My bread and pastry flour can be used in all recipes to replace the all-purpose flour if you are intolerant to corn or salicylates. This flour is lighter and drier so if you are using it for cakes, 1 tablespoon of almond meal or other nut meal to each 100g of flour will increase the moisture level.

LOLA'S ALL-PURPOSE FLOUR

400g BESAN FLOUR

(Known also as chickpea/gram/channa dahl/dahl flour.)

400g MAIZE CORNFLOUR

200g POTATO FLOUR

(Often called potato starch.)

200g YELLOW MAIZE FLOUR

(Also called stone ground maize flour, it is polenta ground to a flour.)

METHOD: See easy blending method, page 11

LOLA'S BREAD AND PASTRY FLOUR

400g BESAN FLOUR

(Known also as chickpea/gram/channa dahl/dahl flour.)

400g POTATO FLOUR

(Sometimes called potato starch.)

200g FINE RICE FLOUR

(Use the finest grind you can find.)

200g ARROWROOT

(Tapioca starch can be used instead of arrowroot.)

METHOD: EASY BLENDING.

You need two large plastic bags and a pasta or sauce strainer about 20cm in diameter.

1. Weigh the ingredients and toss them into a large plastic bag.
2. Give the bag a good shake.
3. Place the strainer in the second bag.
4. Tip the flour into the strainer in the bag and shake the strainer to sift it.

The flour is now ready for use.
Store it in a paper or calico bag so that the flour can breathe.
Two tea towels stitched together with a string tie makes a good flour bag that can be easily laundered. Stored this way the flour will keep in good condition for several years.

Do not keep this flour airtight or it will quickly go mouldy and become rancid. The moisture then will attract insects. A loose-lidded or flip-top container is suitable as long as the flour can obtain some air. All wheat flour is packed in paper or cloth.

BATTER, BREAD AND PASTA

APPLE AND SULTANA SPICE BUN

INGREDIENTS

200mL COLD WATER
1 tsp SALT
3 tbsp CASTER SUGAR
1 tbsp GELATINE
60g MASHED POTATO
1 tbsp INSTANT DRY YEAST (FERMIPAN RECOMMENDED)
200g LOLA'S BREAD AND PASTRY FLOUR (PAGE 11)
70g ARROWROOT
1 tbsp GROUND GINGER
1 tbsp MIXED SPICE
1 tsp CINNAMON
2 EGGS
1 CHOPPED APPLE
150g SULTANAS

PREPARATION

Place the cold water into a large glass bowl or microwave dish.
Add the salt, caster sugar and gelatine; let stand for 1 minute to soften.
Grease a ring or saddle tin with some dairy-free margarine.
Heat the gelatine mixture in the microwave for 50 seconds.

MIXING

Whisk the mashed potato in to the warm gelatine mixture.
Stir in the yeast and let stand for 3 minutes.
Combine the flour, arrowroot and spices.
Tip the dry ingredients into the wet mixture and beat in the whisked eggs.
Beat the mixture for 1 minute with the electric mixer.

BAKING

Set the oven temperature to 180ºC.
Pour a quarter of the mixture into the bread pan and spread over the base.
Sprinkle a quarter of the apple and sultanas over the mixture and top with more batter.
Cover the remaining fruit with more bun mixture.
Leave to stand for 15 minutes. Place in the centre of the oven and bake for 35 minutes.
Remove from the oven and wrap in a tea towel and leave to cool.

*Bake in a Yorkshire pudding tray
set of 4 x 10cm*

YORKSHIRE PUDDING

INGREDIENTS

¼ cup OLIVE OIL
1 EGG
¼ cup WARM WATER
2 tsp GLUTEN-FREE BAKING POWDER
½ tsp SALT
100g LOLA'S BREAD AND PASTRY FLOUR (PAGE 11)

PREPARATION

Set the oven temperature to 200°C.
Place the oil in the Yorkshire pudding trays or a baking dish and place in the hot oven until 'smoking' hot. If you wish to bake the mixture in your roasting pan, to avoid cooking in saturated fat, first remove the cooked roast, drain the surplus fat, add olive oil and heat again before pouring in the batter.

MIXING

Whisk the egg until thick and creamy. Add the warm water, baking powder, salt and flour. Whisk again until smooth. Set aside for a few minutes until the oil is smoking hot.

BAKING

Pour into the pans containing hot oil and bake about 10–15 minutes, until crisp and golden.

FETTUCCINI WITH TOMATO SAUCE

INGREDIENTS

¼ cup WATER

½ cup FROZEN OR BLANCHED FRESH SPINACH (OPTIONAL)

1 tbsp PSYLLIUM HUSKS

1 tsp GELATINE

3 EGGS

1 tbsp OLIVE OIL

300g (+ 50g FOR ROLLING) LOLA'S BREAD AND PASTRY FLOUR (PAGE 11)

PREPARATION

Place the water in a bowl. Using a blender, process the spinach into the water until there are no visible pieces and you have a green liquid; add the psyllium and gelatine and let stand for 5 minutes.

MIXING

Add the eggs and oil to a food processor with the softened psyllium and gelatine mix.
Blend in 300g of the flour. Turn onto a lightly oiled plastic sheet and knead in the remaining flour. Cover and rest 1 hour.

MAKING THE PASTA

Divide the mixture into four; commence rolling one part, keeping the other pieces moist in a plastic bag.
Using a pasta machine, process the pastry by rolling through the machine.
Fold into three, then lightly flour the underside and roll again, making sure that the folded edges are at the side of the machine to give a neat edge. Repeat the process 6 times before making shapes.
Cut with the fettuccini cutter of the pasta machine.
Wrap the fettuccini loosely around your fingers to form a nest; dry on a tea towel overnight.
The pasta can be stored for about 2 weeks in an airtight container when dry or just refrigerated in a plastic bag if you wish to use it fresh without drying.

COOKING THE PASTA

Use plenty of heavily salted water to cook the pasta. Bring to the boil, add the pasta and cook for about 5 minutes. Do not stir. Turn off the heat and leave to stand until the pasta is tender.
Lift the pasta carefully from the water with a pasta scoop and top with your favourite sauce.

Serve with green salad and sour cream
for a delicious entrée.

DEEP-FRIED MUSHROOMS

INGREDIENTS

1 EGG
65mL COLD WATER
1 tsp GLUTEN-FREE BAKING POWDER
100g LOLA'S BREAD AND PASTRY FLOUR (PAGE 11)
1 tsp PEPPER
1 tsp SALT
250g FRESH BUTTON MUSHROOMS
500mL OLIVE OIL FOR FRYING

MIXING

Whisk together the egg and cold water.
Toss in the flour, baking powder, salt and pepper.
Whisk the mixture until it forms a smooth batter.
Leave to stand for 5 minutes.

COOKING

Heat the olive oil in a deep saucepan.
Dip each mushroom into the batter. Using tongs or a fork, lower the mushrooms, one at a time, into the hot oil.
Cook until pale golden, turn if necessary and when cooked drain on kitchen paper.

You will need a set of 6 large muffin pans to cook these buns along with the batter for 1 batch of potato bread. See potato bread recipe recipe on page 30.

FILLED LUNCH BUNS

FILLING

1 SMALL ONION, SLICED
½ GREEN CAPSICUM, CHOPPED
2 tbsp CHOPPED HAM OR BACON
½ cup CANNED CORN KERNELS

AFTER MIXING THE BREAD

Let the potato bread batter stand for 5 minutes. Preheat the oven to 200°C.

Whisk again and spoon 1 tablespoon of batter into each pan, spreading up the side a little to prevent the filling sticking to the tin.

Top the batter with 1 tablespoon corn and small amount of onion, capsicum and ham.

Cover with another tablespoon of batter. Top with poppy seeds if desired.

Leave to rise for 10 minutes before baking. Sprinkle with poppy seeds.

Bake for 15 minutes.

BASIC RECIPE
This pasta is free of corn, wheat, soy, gluten and dairy.
I use a pasta-rolling machine for this recipe; the pasta can
be made by hand but a lot of rolling and folding is needed
for a good result. These little bows are simple to start
with, just use a fluted pizza cutter to cut strips, then cut
bow-sized pieces and pinch in the centre.

GLUTEN-FREE PASTA

INGREDIENTS

$\frac{1}{4}$ cup WATER
1 tbsp PSYLLIUM HUSKS
1 tsp GELATINE
3 EGGS
1 tbsp OLIVE OIL
300g (+ 50g FOR ROLLING) LOLA'S BREAD AND PASTRY FLOUR (PAGE 11)

PREPARATION

Place the water in a bowl and add the psyllium and gelatine.

MIXING

Add the eggs and oil to a food processor with the softened psyllium and gelatine mix.
Blend in 300g of the flour.
Turn onto a lightly oiled plastic sheet and knead in the remaining flour. Cover and rest for 1 hour.

MAKING THE PASTA

Divide the mixture into four; commence rolling one part, keeping the other pieces moist in a plastic bag.
Using a pasta machine, process the pastry by rolling through the machine.
Fold into three, lightly flour the underside and roll again, making sure that the folded edges are at the side of the machine to give a neat edge.
Repeat the process six times before making shapes.
Dry the finished pasta on a clean tea towel overnight to store for a few weeks or keep in the refrigerator to cook in the next few days.

Bake in a 28 x 12 x 10cm tin.

HI-FIBRE YEAST-FREE LOAF

INGREDIENTS

1 tbsp GELATINE
2 tbsp PSYLLIUM HUSKS
500g LOLA'S BREAD AND PASTRY FLOUR (PAGE 11)
3 tbsp GLUTEN-FREE BAKING POWDER
3 EGG WHITES
2 tsp SALT
1 tsp SUGAR
2 tbsp OLIVE OIL

PREPARATION

Place $\frac{1}{2}$ cup cold water in a small bowl and sprinkle the gelatine over it. Let stand until the gelatine sinks; heat the mixture in the microwave 20 seconds on high.
Place $1\frac{1}{4}$ cups cold water into small bowl and sprinkle the psyllium on top; whisk in.
Leave to stand for about 2 minutes until the mixture is thick.
Grease a large bread tin and line it with baking paper.
Combine the flour and baking powder.

MIXING

Beat the egg whites, salt and sugar until stiff, then spoon the warm gelatine mixture into the beaten egg whites, a little at a time; this should be like meringue.
Fold the psyllium mixture into the beaten egg whites.
Add the oil and the dry ingredients and beat for 1 minute with an electric mixer.
Pour into the prepared bread tin; let stand for 10 minutes.

BAKING

While the mixture is standing, preheat the oven to 200ºC.
Cook in the centre of the oven for 50–60 minutes.
Remove from the tin and wrap in a damp cloth.

This mixture can be baked in one or two tins depending on the thickness of the bread required. You can produce a reasonable result by replacing the egg with a double quantity of an egg substitute.

HERB FOCACCIA BREAD

INGREDIENTS

1 tsp GELATINE
2 tsp PSYLLIUM
$\frac{1}{2}$ cup COLD WATER
65mL OLIVE OIL
1 EGG
140g LOLA'S BREAD AND PASTRY FLOUR (PAGE 11)
$\frac{1}{2}$ tsp SALT
1 tsp SUGAR
1 tsp MIXED HERBS
1 tbsp DRIED YEAST
1 tsp SESAME SEEDS

PREPARATION

Place the gelatine and psyllium into the cold water and let stand for 2 minutes.
Grease the sides of one or two 20cm sandwich pans and cut a circle of baking paper to line the bottom of the pan.
Heat the gelatine and psyllium mix in the microwave until clear (about 20 seconds).

MIXING

Place the oil and egg into a large mixing bowl. Beat with a rotary whisk.
Add the warm gelatine mixture to the egg and oil. Fold in the flour, salt, sugar, herbs and yeast.
Beat the mixture with a rotary whisk for about 1 minute to make sure the yeast is well distributed. Pour the batter into the prepared sandwich pans and leave the mixture to stand for 40 minutes until bubbles form; it does not rise much in the pan.

BAKING

Preheat the oven to 220°C.
Sprinkle the top of the bread dough with sesame seeds and cook for 10 minutes.

SERVING

Split through, spread with butter and use as you would any bread. It can be toasted or frozen. It is very good for lunches.
Note: Ensure that you use Lola's Bread & Pastry Flour. Other flours use mostly cornflour which absorbs water and will make too thick to pour.

Makes six large buns.

HOT CROSS BUNS

INGREDIENTS

250mL COLD WATER
2 tsp SALT
100g CASTER SUGAR
1 tbsp GELATINE
2 tbsp GLYCERINE
2 tbsp MARGARINE
2 tbsp INSTANT DRY YEAST
 (FERMIPAN RECOMMENDED)
300g LOLA'S BREAD AND PASTRY
FLOUR (SEE PAGE 11)

100g ARROWROOT
60g GROUND ALMONDS (ALMOND MEAL)
1 tbsp MIXED SPICE
1 tbsp CINNAMON
2 tsp GROUND GINGER
1 EGG
$\frac{1}{2}$ cup MIXED DRIED FRUIT

PREPARATION

Place the cold water, salt, sugar and gelatine in a large glass bowl or microwave dish.
Let stand for 1 minute to soften. Heat in the microwave for 40 seconds.
Grease muffin tins or bun trays with some dairy-free margarine or cooking spray.
Add the glycerine and margarine to the gelatine mixture.

MIXING

Stir in the yeast and whisk slightly. Let stand for 3 minutes.
Place the flour, arrowroot, almond meal and spices in a plastic bag and give a good shake
to mix well.
Lightly whisk the egg. Tip the dry ingredients into the yeast mixture and add the egg.
Beat the mixture for 2 minutes with an electric mixer.
Let stand for 10 minutes. Whisk for 30 seconds.
For easier filling of bun tins, pour the mixture into a jug. Stand the mixture for another 10
minutes, then whisk again. Note: The second rising refines the texture.

BAKING

Preheat the oven to 180°C.

Quarter fill the bun pans with the mixture.

Sprinkle about 1 teaspoonful of fruit over the mixture and top with more batter.

Sprinkle the remaining fruit over each bun and top with a small amount of batter.

Leave to stand for 15 minutes, until a few bubbles appear.

Pipe crosses on top of each bun.

Place in the centre of the oven and bake for 30 minutes.

Glaze with bun glaze as soon as the buns are cooked – while they are still hot.

CROSS MIX

Sprinkle 2 teaspoons of psyllium on $^1/_4$ cup cold water and let stand to thicken.

Add 1 tablespoon sugar and 1 tablespoon fine rice flour. Pipe on the uncooked buns.

BUN GLAZE

$^1/_4$ cup COLD WATER

1 tbsp GELATINE

2 tbsp SUGAR

1 tsp MIXED SPICE

Boil together for 1 minute. Brush buns as directed.

FOIL BUN CUPS

These buns were cooked in foil cups made by cutting 20cm squares of foil.

Turn in 2cm around the square and press down.

Shape the cup using a plastic golden syrup container or square jar as a mould.

Bring up four sides and crease corners, press the corners to each side and secure with sticky tape. Spray inside of each cup with cooking spray.

The cooked pizza will freeze well.

MEDITERRANEAN PIZZA

INGREDIENTS

For 2 x 20cm or 1 large base:
80mL HOT WATER
65mL OLIVE OIL
140g LOLA'S BREAD AND
PASTRY FLOUR (PAGE 11)

1 tsp SALT
1 tsp SUGAR
1 tbsp DRIED YEAST

PREPARATION

Grease the sides of small trays to prevent filling sticking to the tins. If you want to freeze the bases, cut some baking paper to line the bottom of each pan; this can then be left on for freezing to prevent the base drying.

Prepare the topping.

MIXING

Place the hot water into a mixing bowl.

Add the oil and fold in the flour, salt, sugar and yeast.

Beat the mixture with a rotary whisk for about 1 minute to make sure the yeast is well distributed.

Pour the batter into the prepared tins.

Leave the mixture to stand for 30 minutes, until the mixture shows a few bubbles.

Preheat the oven to 220ºC.

Place the topping on top of the uncooked batter and cook for about 20 minutes or until the pizza is firm to touch. If you like a crisp pastry, bake the crust for 10 minutes before adding the topping.

If you are freezing the bases cook them for about 10 minutes only or until they are just firm to touch, to prevent drying when the topping is finally added.

TOPPING

1 can ITALIAN PEELED TOMATOES
HERBS AND ONION TO TASTE
SLICED CAPSICUM, SLICES OF SALAMI OR PEPPERONI, BLACK OLIVES, ANCHOVIES, CHILLIES
50g GRATED TASTY CHEESE

Cook the tomatoes on a high heat to reduce the liquid and increase the flavour.

Add the herbs, sliced onion and capsicum and spread onto the uncooked batter.

Place the salami and olives on top and sprinkle with the grated cheese.

Tip: Frozen bases should be foil-wrapped to prevent freezer burn.

This bread mixture is a light batter, but to make the large loaf you will need a large electric mixer. If you only have a hand mixer you can make half the quantity in a small tin. The large mixer is required to efficiently blend the yeast through the mixture. This takes the place of kneading in wheat bread. It is much easier to make this loaf if you replace the egg whites with a product such as my gluten-free bread improver that is basically dried egg white and citric acid. This then eliminates the need for whisking the egg whites and separately dissolving gelatine. You can just throw all ingredients into the warm water and mix. To make a square sandwich loaf use a flat scone tray as a lid for the bread tin.

SANDWICH BREAD

INGREDIENTS

2 tbsp GELATINE
375mL COLD WATER
125mL BOILING WATER
1 tsp SUGAR
2 tbsp DRIED YEAST

3 EGG WHITES
1 tsp SALT
450g LOLA'S BREAD AND PASTRY FLOUR (PAGE 11)
50g ARROWROOT
125mL OLIVE OIL

PREPARATION

Grease a large loaf tin 28 x 12 x 10cm deep and line it with baking paper.

Place the gelatine into 250mL of the cold water and let it soak until it sinks.

Heat the gelatine mixture in a microwave until it is clear (about 1 minute). Set aside to cool.

Place 125mL of cold water and 125mL boiling water in a small bowl; add the sugar and yeast. It will become frothy in a few minutes.

MIXING

Whisk the egg whites with the salt until stiff.

While beating the egg whites, add the gelatine mixture a spoonful at a time.

Remove from the mixer, sift the flour and arrowroot into the egg mixture and fold in the frothy yeast, then the oil.

Whisk the mixture with a wire whisk to ensure that the ingredients are blended.

Cover the basin with plastic wrap and leave the bread mixture to stand in the basin for about 15 minutes until the mixture is 'puffy' – the time is dependent on the quality of the yeast.

Whisk and repeat the process after the second rising. Whisk again and pour into the prepared bread tin. Cover and let stand for 20–30 minutes to rise, until it is about an inch from top of tin; it will continue to rise in the oven.

Preheat the oven to 200°C.

BAKING

Place the bread on the lowest shelf in your oven and after 10 minutes place a scone tray on top of the tin to give a square sandwich loaf that is easy to slice.

Bake the bread for 1 hour.

Remove from the oven and cool in the tin before slicing.

Tip: An electric knife is helpful for slicing gluten-free bread. This loaf freezes well but as with all bread and cakes it should be wrapped in foil to prevent freezer burn.

This recipe does not contain yeast, but still makes two good pizza bases.

YEAST-FREE PIZZA

INGREDIENTS

65mL WARM WATER
2 tbsp OLIVE OIL
1 EGG
1 tbsp GELATINE
160g LOLA'S BREAD AND PASTRY FLOUR (PAGE 11)
1 tsp SALT
1 tsp GLUTEN-FREE BAKING POWDER
50g MASHED POTATO

PREPARATION

Grease the sides of 2 x 20cm sandwich pans and cut a circle of baking paper to line the bottom of each pan.
Preheat the oven to 200°C.
Prepare the topping for the pizza.

MIXING

Place the warm water, oil and lightly whisked egg into a bowl and sift in the gelatine, flour, salt and baking powder.
Add the mashed potato and beat the mixture with a rotary whisk for about 1 minute.
Pour the batter into the two prepared cake tins. Let stand for 10 minutes.

BAKING

Place the topping on top of the batter and cook for about 10 minutes or until the pizza is firm.
If you prefer a crunchy crust, partially bake the crust before adding the topping.

TOPPING

250g MUSHROOMS
1 tbsp BUTTER
100g CHOPPED HAM
100g GRATED MOZZARELLA CHEESE
OLIVES AND CAPSICUM TO GARNISH

Sauté the mushrooms in the butter until they are soft; arrange on top of the batter.
Top with the chopped ham and grated cheese and garnish with olives and capsicum.
Tip: Gluten-free rice crumbs mixed with melted dairy-free margarine can replace cheese.
Pinenuts are good for added flavour.

One of my most popular recipes, potato bread is made by beginners in all of my cooking classes. It can be made in a rib-bottomed saddle tin or in a small deep bread tin. This mixture is meant to be a quick, easy bread for eating the same day as all bread once was. If you wish to keep it longer or freeze it, it is necessary to beat it again after the initial 15 minute rise and let it rise again, then beat and leave for another 20 minutes before baking.

POTATO BREAD

INGREDIENTS

1 tbsp GELATINE
200mL COLD WATER
65g SOFT MASHED POTATO
50g ARROWROOT
65mL ($\frac{1}{4}$ cup) OLIVE OIL

1 tsp SUGAR
1 tsp SALT
1 tbsp DRIED YEAST
200g LOLA'S BREAD AND PASTRY FLOUR (PAGE 11)
1 EGG

PREPARATION

Place the gelatine into the cold water and let stand to soften.
Preheat the oven to 200ºC.
Select a 23 x 8 x 7cm deep bread tin to cook the loaf. Bread cooks best in tin, not aluminium. If it is a new tin, line it with baking paper or grease it well. Seasoned tins don't need to be greased unless to hold seeds.

MIXING

When the gelatine has softened, heat the mixture over low heat until clear.
Tip the hot gelatine mixture into the mashed potato and mix well.
Add the olive oil, sugar and salt to this mixture and while it is still warm add the yeast.
Sift in the flour and add the unbeaten egg or egg-replacer mix.
Beat the mixture with an electric beater for about 1 minute. (The mixture should be a thick batter, add more warm water if too stiff.)
Pour the batter into the prepared tin and let it stand for 10–15 minutes, or until the mixture is half an inch from top of tin, it will continue to rise in the oven.

BAKING

Sprinkle with sesame seeds and place in the centre of the oven.
Cook for about 40 minutes or until the loaf sounds hollow when tapped.

A FEW TIPS

- If you want a square loaf, place a greased scone tray on top of the bread tin and allow another 10 minutes of cooking.
- Gluten- and wheat-free breads are made from batter rather than dough as yeast reacts in a different manner when there is no gluten in the flour. It is important to catch the rising yeast at just the right time; if you leave it to rise too long the bread will collapse in the oven.
- If your bread sticks to the tin it needs extra baking or a slightly hotter oven. An oven thermometer is much cheaper than a service if you are doubtful about your oven. The thermometer should give the accurate temperature of your oven after 20 minutes.
- Some brands of dried yeast do not give a good result with gluten-free flour. I use Fermipan, a commercial grade of yeast used by bakers worldwide.

*Serve with ice cream or
creamy caramel sauce (page 149).*

BANANA FRITTERS

INGREDIENTS

1 EGG
1 tbsp CASTER SUGAR
65mL WATER
150g LOLA'S ALL-PURPOSE FLOUR (PAGE 10)
1 tsp GLUTEN-FREE BAKING POWDER
OLIVE OIL FOR FRYING
2 or 3 SMALL BANANAS
SUGAR FOR SPRINKLING

PREPARATION

Break the egg into a bowl and beat together with the sugar and water.
Sift in the flour and baking powder and whisk to a smooth batter.
Heat the oil in a deep pan.
Coat each banana with the batter and gently place in the hot oil.
Cook until golden, then remove and drain on kitchen paper.
Sprinkle with sugar and serve with ice cream.

CAKES FOR ALL OCCASIONS

*This moist rich chocolate
cake is a dairy-free delight.
Tip: A smear of oil on the scales will
make golden syrup slide off easily.*

CHOCOLATE MUD CAKE

INGREDIENTS

500g SWEET POTATO
180g GOLDEN SYRUP
125mL OLIVE OIL
1 tbsp WATER
2 EGGS
200g SUGAR
50g COCOA
1 tbsp GLUTEN-FREE BAKING POWDER
1 tsp BICARBONATE OF SODA
300g LOLA'S ALL-PURPOSE FLOUR (PAGE 10)

PREPARATION

Peel the sweet potatoes and cook in the microwave with a little water in a covered casserole dish, or boil on the stove in the usual way.
Preheat the oven to 180°C.
Grease a large loaf pan with margarine and line the bottom with baking paper.

MIXING

Mash or blend the cooked sweet potato in a saucepan and add the syrup, olive oil and water to the blended potato.
Beat the eggs and sugar over a saucepan of hot water until the mixture is warm and shows a few frothy bubbles. Place on an electric mixer or beat with a rotary beater until thick and creamy.
Sift the cocoa, baking powder, bicarbonate of soda and flour carefully into the mixture.
Finally, add the cake batter to the sweet potato mixture and blend with a wire whisk.

BAKING

Pour into the prepared pan and place in the centre of the oven for 50 minutes.
Cool in the tin before icing.
Ice with chocolate fudge icing and decorate with grapes dipped in melted chocolate.

FUDGE ICING

Warm together 80g brown sugar, 125g butter, 2 tablespoons cocoa and 1 teaspoon vanilla essence. When it has caramelised, add enough sifted pure icing sugar (about 100g) to make a thick rich icing.
Tip: A chocolate syrup made from half a cup each of sugar and water and 1 tablespoon of cocoa or melted chocolate warmed can be spooned over the hot cake for a more moist cake.

CHOCOLATE WEDDING (OR BIRTHDAY) CAKE

MODIFICATION TO CHOCOLATE MUD CAKE

This is a delicious modification to my chocolate mud cake on page 36.

This recipe fills a 23cm round loose-based cheesecake tin. The tin needs to be three quarters full. This cake was cooked on Friday morning, and was still moist on Monday, making it suitable for a chocolate wedding cake.

PREPARATION

Add 200g melted dark cooking chocolate to the sweet potato and golden syrup mix.
I use large size eggs, and no further liquid is needed.
Add 50g ground almonds to the cocoa and flour mixture. I use all-purpose flour and 1 tablespoon carob to make the cake a little darker.
Because of the chocolate it is necessary to reduce the oven temperature to 150°C and cook for 1 hour.
When the cake is cooked, carefully spoon over the hot cake $\frac{1}{2}$ cup brandy or port, or a mixture of each.
Leave to cool in the tin.
Place a board on top of the tin and turn upside down when cool to make sure that the liquor does not all soak to the bottom, which will become the top for decorating.

MELTING CHOCOLATE

When you are melting chocolate it is most important to follow a few rules:
One drop of water or steam will ruin your chocolate and you will have to start again.
Break the chocolate into pieces or use dark buttons.
Bring some water to the boil in a saucepan and remove from the heat.
Place the chocolate in a bowl over the hot water and cover the bowl with a plate to prevent any steam mixing with the chocolate.

EASY FRUIT CAKE

INGREDIENTS

2 EGGS
1kg MIXED FRUIT AND CHOPPED NUTS (YOUR FAVOURITE MIXTURE)
125g each BUTTER AND BROWN SUGAR
150g LOLA'S ALL-PURPOSE FLOUR (PAGE 10)
1 tbsp GELATINE
1 tbsp MIXED SPICES
TOPPING: GLACÉ CHERRIES, NUTS, DRIED APRICOTS AND PINEAPPLE
3 tbsp RUM OR BRANDY

PREPARATION

Grease and line the tin with baking paper.
Preheat the oven to 160°C.
Whisk the eggs with a hand whisk.
Select your fruit and nuts and chop any large pieces.

MIXING

Lightly cream the butter and sugar; over beating will cause the fruit to sink.
Mix flour, gelatine and spices into the bowl of prepared fruit.
Add the fruit and flour mix to the creamed sugar and butter.
Add the eggs to the mixture, turning carefully with a wooden spoon.
Spoon the mixture into the prepared tin and arrange the 'topping' fruits and nuts on the cake.

BAKING

Bake on the low shelf for 2–2$\frac{1}{2}$ hours, depending on the depth of the tin.
Remove from the oven and sprinkle the spirit evenly over the cake. Return to the warm oven to cool in the tin.

FAIRY CAKES

INGREDIENTS

4 EGGS
200g CASTER SUGAR
200g LOLA'S ALL-PURPOSE FLOUR (PAGE 10)
50g GROUND ALMONDS
1 tbsp VANILLA ESSENCE
2 tbsp PSYLLIUM
2 tbsp GELATINE
3 tsps GLUTEN-FREE BAKING POWDER
200g BUTTER OR MARGARINE
ICING OR CREAM, AS DESIRED, FOR DECORATION

PREPARATION

Line 24 patty tins with papers. Don't use aluminum tins.
Preheat the oven to 180°C.

MIXING

Place the ingredients, except the icing, into a mixing bowl in their listed order and mix well with an electric mixer for about 1 minute. Spoon into the prepared patty pans and let rest for 5 minutes to help with the rising of the cakes.

BAKING

Place on the high shelf in your oven and bake for 10 minutes until just firm to touch; don't overcook. Ice or fill with cream as desired.

FREEZING

Cakes will retain their moisture for several days kept in a cake tin and will freeze well in foil or a plastic container. They will dry in the freezer in a plastic bag.

HI-FIBRE CARROT SLICE

INGREDIENTS

200g LOLA'S ALL-PURPOSE FLOUR (PAGE 10)
2 tsp GLUTEN-FREE BAKING POWDER
1 tbsp GELATINE
1 tbsp PSYLLIUM
2 tsp MIXED SPICE
50g DESICCATED COCONUT
110g FINELY GRATED CARROT
110g SULTANAS
170g BROWN SUGAR
125mL OLIVE OIL
2 tsp VANILLA ESSENCE
3 EGGS

PREPARATION

Preheat the oven to 180ºC.
Grease the slab pan and line the bottom with baking paper.
Lightly whisk the eggs.

MIXING

Combine the flour, baking powder, gelatine, psyllium, spices, coconut, carrot and sultanas.
Place the brown sugar, oil and vanilla essence in a large saucepan and warm slightly.
Remove from the heat and add all the other ingredients, alternating the dry ingredients with the eggs.
Combine well and spoon into the baking tin.

BAKING

Bake in the centre shelf of the oven for 25 minutes.
Leave to cool in the tin.
When cold, ice with lemon frosting.

LEMON FROSTING

250g SIFTED PURE ICING SUGAR
1 tbsp BUTTER
1 tbsp LEMON JUICE
Whisk ingredients together well and use to top the cooled cake.

LOLA'S CHRISTMAS CAKE

INGREDIENTS

500g SULTANAS
500g RAISINS
375g MIXED FRUIT
50g SLIVERED ALMONDS
50g CHOPPED PECAN NUTS
125g RED, GREEN AND YELLOW GLACÉ CHERRIES
125g CHOPPED DATES
125g PRUNES, CHOPPED
ZEST OF 1 LEMON
250g CHOPPED GLACÉ FRUITS (sprinkle with 100mL rum or brandy, cover and stand overnight.)

NEXT DAY

Place in a sieve:
300g LOLA'S ALL-PURPOSE FLOUR (PAGE 10)
1 tsp GINGER
1 level tsp BICARBONATE SODA
1 tsp CINNAMON
2 tsp MIXED SPICE
2 tsp NUTMEG

INTO THE MIXER BOWL

250g BUTTER
1 tsp PLUM JAM
250g BROWN SUGAR
1 tsp TREACLE
Into another basin:
Break 5 eggs and hand whisk them lightly.

TOPPING (OPTIONAL)

250g GLACÉ FRUITS: PEACH,
PINEAPPLE, 125g RED, GREEN AND YELLOW GLACÉ CHERRIES
If you have measured all those ingredients, now comes the easy part.

To simplify this recipe, use 2 kg of your favourite fruit and nut mixture.

PREPARATION

Grease your cake tin to hold the paper in place and line it with baking paper.
Place the oven shelf to the lowest position in the oven.
Preheat the oven to 180°C.

MIXING

Mix, don't beat the butter and sugar; over-beating will cause the fruit to sink.
Sift the flour and spices into the bowl of prepared fruit. Mix with a wooden spoon or your hands until the fruit is coated with flour. Add the fruit and flour mix to the creamed sugar and butter. Stir in the eggs and turn the mixture with a wooden spoon.

BAKING

Spoon the mixture into the cake tin and decorate the top with nuts and glacé fruits.
Cover the top of the cake with a sheet of foil to prevent the nuts from burning.
Reduce the temperature to 160°C and place the cake on the lower shelf of the oven.
Cook for 3 hours, or $2\frac{1}{2}$ hours if cooked in a shallow tin.
When the cake is cooked, remove from the oven. If you think it needs a little more time, turn off the oven and leave it in the oven to cool.
Wrap the cooled cake in a cloth and store in the cupboard. Do not refrigerate as this prevents the cake from maturing.
Do not cut the cake for at least 24 hours and preferably not for 7 days.

This cake will retain moisture for several days if kept in a closed container.

ORANGE POPPY SEED LOG

INGREDIENTS

3 EGGS
150g CASTER SUGAR
150g LOLA'S ALL-PURPOSE FLOUR (PAGE 11)
80g GROUND ALMONDS
GRATED RIND OF 2 ORANGES
2 tbsp PSYLLIUM
1 tbsp GELATINE
2 tbsp POPPY SEEDS
2 tsp GLUTEN-FREE BAKING POWDER
150g BUTTER
125mL ORANGE JUICE

PREPARATION

Preheat the oven to 180°C. Grease heavily a 30cm log pan with margarine.

MIXING

Place all the ingredients into a mixing bowl in their listed order and mix well with an electric mixer for about 1 minute and scrape into the prepared pan.

BAKING

Place on the middle shelf in your oven and bake for 35 minutes until just firm to touch.
Remove from the oven and, while it is still in the tin, sprinkle the warm orange juice over the cake. Stand for a few minutes before turning out.
When cool ice with orange icing.

ORANGE ICING

2 cups PURE ICING SUGAR
JUICE OF 1 ORANGE
2 tbsp BUTTER OR MARGARINE
Cream together and spread on the cooled cake.

This light fluffy sponge makes a great birthday cake.

PASSIONFRUIT SPONGE

INGREDIENTS

1 tbsp MARGARINE
3 tbsp BOILING WATER
4 EGGS
150g CASTER SUGAR
150g LOLA'S ALL-PURPOSE FLOUR (PAGE 10)
4 tsp GLUTEN-FREE BAKING POWDER

PASSIONFRUIT ICING

2 cups PURE ICING SUGAR, SIEVED
1 tbsp BOILING WATER
3 tbsp MARGARINE
2 PASSIONFRUIT

PREPARATION

Preheat the oven at 180ºC.

Place the margarine into a small bowl and add the boiling water; leave to melt.

Grease the sides of 2 x 20cm flan tins and dust with gluten-free flour mixture. Line the bottom with baking paper.

Note: Do not use aluminium pans as your sponge will not cook evenly; it will cook at the edges before the centre, giving you a dry result.

MIXING

Hand whisk the eggs and caster sugar over hot water until they are just warm and bubbly.

Using an electric mixer, beat until the mixture is thick and creamy.

Sift the flour and baking powder and fold into the egg mixture.

Pour the water–margarine mixture down the inside of the bowl.

Fold the mixture with a wire whisk, being careful not to over mix as this will release the air and flatten the sponge.

Pour into the tin and gently move the mixture with a spatula so that a small depression is made in the centre of the cake.

BAKING

Place in the centre of the preheated oven and cook for 15 minutes.

Turn off the oven and stand for 5 minutes in the oven before removing and turning out.

If the mixture will not pour from the tin, it is too dry; add a little more warm water.

DECORATING THE CAKE

Combine the icing ingredients and pour on the top of one cake.

Fill the cake with whipped cream, softened creamed ricotta cheese or patisserie custard.

Note: Unfilled cakes freeze well if foil-wrapped. They will dry if only plastic-wrapped.

No cake or biscuit crumbs are needed to make this recipe. The rum balls can be chocolate-coated or for a dairy-free result, roll in cocoa or coconut.

RUM BALLS

INGREDIENTS

60g DAIRY-FREE MARGARINE
2 tbsp TREACLE
60g BROWN SUGAR
1 tbsp COCOA
1 tbsp RUM
2 tbsp ALMOND MEAL
1 cup MIXED CHOPPED RAISINS AND PRUNES
1 cup CHOPPED MIXED NUTS: FLAKED ALMONDS, CASHEWS, WALNUTS AND HAZELNUTS

METHOD

Place the margarine, treacle and brown sugar in a saucepan and slowly bring to the boil. Remove from the heat and stir in the remaining ingredients. Mix well by hand or in a food processor. Cool and roll into balls. Coat as desired (see above).

TRADITIONAL LAMINGTONS

INGREDIENTS

1 tsp BUTTER
1 tsp VANILLA ESSENCE
3 tsp HOT WATER
3 LARGE EGGS

100g CASTER SUGAR
100g LOLA'S ALL-PURPOSE FLOUR (PAGE 10)
1 tsp GLUTEN-FREE BAKING POWDER

PREPARATION

Preheat the oven to 160°C.
Prepare a 20cm square tin by greasing the sides with margarine and placing a layer of baking paper in the bottom of the tin.
Place the butter in a small bowl, add the vanilla essence and hot water, and let stand for 1 minute.

MIXING

Place the eggs and caster sugar in a metal bowl and whisk with a wire whisk over a saucepan of hot water until the mixture is warm and slightly frothy. Remove from the heat and continue beating with a rotary or electric beater until the mixture is thick and creamy but not stiff.
Carefully sift the flour and baking powder into the egg mixture. Pour the warm liquid around the sides of the bowl as you continue to fold the mixture.

BAKING

Quickly pour into the prepared cake tin and place in the centre of the oven.
Cook for 15 minutes. Let stand in the oven for an extra 5 minutes with the door ajar.

FINISHING LAMINGTONS

Cool the cake and cut into squares.
Freeze the squares for about 20 minutes before coating with chocolate icing.
Finish by rolling the coated squares in desiccated coconut.

CHOCOLATE ICING

200g PURE ICING SUGAR
1 tbsp COCOA
1 tsp BUTTER

BOILING WATER TO MIX
150g DESICCATED COCONUT
1 tsp VANILLA ESSENCE

Sift the cocoa and icing sugar together into a large bowl.
Dissolve the butter in a little hot water, add to the icing sugar and mix to a thin icing.
Coat each frozen cake square with the chocolate icing and roll in coconut.
The completed cakes will freeze well.

STRAWBERRY SHORTCAKE

INGREDIENTS

4 EGGS
100g CASTER SUGAR
2 tsp MARGARINE
1 tbsp GLYCERINE
4 tbsp HOT WATER
100g LOLA'S BREAD AND PASTRY FLOUR (PAGE 11)
2 tsp GLUTEN-FREE BAKING POWDER
2 tsp VANILLA ESSENCE

FILLING

150g FRESH STRAWBERRIES
250mL FRESH CREAM

PREPARATION

Preheat the oven to 180°C.
Grease the sides and line the bottom of 2 x 20cm round cake tins with baking paper.

MIXING

Place the eggs and caster sugar in a large metal bowl and hand whisk over a saucepan of hot water until the mixture is slightly warm and frothy.
Remove from the heat and continue beating with a rotary or electric mixer until the mixture is thick and creamy but not stiff.
Add the margarine and glycerine to the hot water and let stand for 1 minute.
Fold in the sifted flours and baking powder to the beaten eggs and sugar.
Mix in the vanilla essence, glycerine, margarine and water. Fold lightly but thoroughly.

BAKING

Pour into the prepared tins, level quickly with a plastic spatula and cook for 30 minutes.
Let stand in the tin for 1 minute before turning onto a wire rack to cool.

FINISHING THE SHORTCAKE

When the cakes are cold, select 8 small strawberries for decoration and set aside.
Slice the remaining strawberries into the whipped cream and fold through to join the cakes.
Pipe 8 rosettes of the whipped cream in a circle on top of the shortcake; place a berry on each rosette.
Dust the top of the shortcake with pure icing sugar.

VANILLA BUTTER CAKE

INGREDIENTS

4 EGGS
200g CASTER SUGAR
180g LOLA'S ALL-PURPOSE FLOUR (PAGE 10)
50g GROUND ALMONDS
1 tbsp VANILLA ESSENCE
2 tbsp PSYLLIUM
2 tbsp GELATINE
3 tsp GLUTEN-FREE BAKING POWDER
200g BUTTER

PREPARATION

Grease a large loaf tin; I use my heavy bread tin (not aluminium) and line it with baking paper.
Preheat the oven to 150ºC.

MIXING

Place the ingredients into a mixing bowl in their listed order and mix well with an electric mixer
for about 1 minute. Scrape into the loaf tin, level and let rest for 5 minutes.

BAKING

Place on the lowest shelf in your oven and bake for 50 minutes until just firm to touch.
Remove from the oven and cool in the tin.
Cover with a clean tea towel to prevent drying.

This cake will retain its moisture for several days in a cake container and is more moist
the next day.

The cake is moist and delicious.

VICKI'S BANANA CAKE

INGREDIENTS

2 EGGS
100g CASTER SUGAR
2 RIPE BANANAS
¼ cup OLIVE OIL
100g LOLA'S ALL-PURPOSE FLOUR (PAGE 10)
1 tbsp PSYLLIUM
2 tsp GLUTEN-FREE BAKING POWDER
1 tsp BICARBONATE OF SODA

PREPARATION

Preheat the oven to 150°C.
Mash the bananas.
Grease a cake tin and line the bottom.

MIXING

Place the eggs and sugar in a bowl and hand whisk over a saucepan of boiling water until the mixture is warm and bubbly.
Remove from the heat and beat with electric beater until thick and creamy.
Add the mashed bananas and oil.
Fold in the dry ingredients and mix well (mixture stays quite 'runny').

BAKING

Pour into the cake tin and bake for 45–55 minutes.
Leave to stand for 5 minutes in the tin before turning out.
When cold, finish with cream cheese frosting.

CREAM CHEESE FROSTING

80g CREAM CHEESE (SOFTENED TO ROOM TEMPERATURE)
3 tsp LEMON JUICE AND SOME ZEST
1 tbsp SOFT MARGARINE
1½ cups PURE ICING SUGAR
Blend ingredients together until smooth.
Spread on to cold cake.
Note: This cake is dairy-free if you use a dairy-free margarine to replace cream cheese and butter in the icing.

COOKIES AND KIDS' THINGS

ALMOND COOKIES

INGREDIENTS

100g LOLA'S ALL-PURPOSE FLOUR (PAGE 10)
1 tsp BICARBONATE OF SODA
100g SUGAR
40g FLAKED ALMONDS
25g GROUND ALMONDS
25g BABY RICE CEREAL
80mL OLIVE OIL
1 tbsp WATER
3 tbsp LIQUID GLUCOSE
3 tsp VANILLA ESSENCE
1 tsp ALMOND ESSENCE

PREPARATION

Preheat the oven to 160°C.
Cover a baking tray with foil or baking paper.

MIXING

Place the flour, sugar, bicarbonate of soda, flaked almonds, ground almonds and rice cereal into a mixing bowl and mix with a wire whisk or fork to combine the ingredients.
Place the oil, water and glucose into a large saucepan and heat slowly to simmer point.
Remove the saucepan from the heat and add the dry ingredients to the oil mixture.
Add the vanilla essence and almond essence and mix well.
Turn onto a plastic sheet and roll in a long sausage shape.
Note: At this stage the cookies can be left in the refrigerator until you wish to cook them. If they are well wrapped they will keep for a week. Remove from refrigerator and leave to reach room temperature before slicing to bake.

BAKING

Slice the sausage shape cookie mixture into 16 portions using a sharp knife, and place on the baking tray.
Cook for about 10–15 minutes until a pale golden colour.
Cool on the tray if possible.

These yummy fingers are meant to be soft like gingerbread. Gingernuts can be made using this recipe if you double the sugar and boil the mixture for a few seconds before adding the dry ingredients.

GINGER FINGERS

INGREDIENTS

100g LOLA'S ALL-PURPOSE FLOUR (PAGE 10)
1 tsp CINNAMON
100g SUGAR
1 tsp NUTMEG
1 tbsp GROUND GINGER
25g BABY RICE CEREAL
1 tsp BICARBONATE OF SODA
25g DESICCATED COCONUT
80mL OLIVE OIL
100g TREACLE
1 tbsp WATER

PREPARATION

Preheat the oven to 160°C.
Line an oven tray with baking paper.

MIXING

Place the dry ingredients into a mixing bowl and stir with a wire whisk to ensure that they are evenly distributed.
Tip the oil, treacle and water into a large saucepan and heat to boiling point.
Remove the saucepan from the heat and add the dry ingredients to the mixture, stirring to combine all the ingredients.
Tip the mixture onto a plastic sheet and press into a long bar shape.

BAKING

Unroll the plastic and, using a knife that has been dipped in olive oil, cut the bars into thick strips.
Lift onto the prepared baking tray with a spatula and press lightly with a fork.
Cook for 10–15 minutes until a deep golden brown.

There is no butter in these crisps so they will keep for many weeks in an airtight container.

CURRANT AND COCONUT CRISPS

INGREDIENTS

3 EGGS
300g CASTER SUGAR
200g LOLA'S ALL-PURPOSE FLOUR (PAGE 10)
125g CURRANTS
150g DESICCATED COCONUT
2 tsp VANILLA ESSENCE

PREPARATION

Grease or cover two large oven trays with baking paper.
Preheat the oven to 160ºC.

MIXING

Place the eggs and sugar in a large bowl and hand whisk over a saucepan of hot water until the mixture is luke warm and frothy.
Remove from the heat and continue beating with a rotary or electric beater until the mixture will hold its shape.
While the mixture is beating, combine the flour with the currants and coconut.
Carefully fold the dry ingredients into the whipped egg mixture; add the vanilla essence.

BAKING

Place teaspoonfuls of mixture onto the prepared trays in rough heaps, leaving plenty of room for the cookies to spread.
Bake for 20 minutes.
Turn the heat off and leave the cookies in the oven for an additional 10 minutes.

ALMOND COOKIES
GINGER FINGERS
CURRANT AND COCONUT CRISPS

This is the recipe that I use for handout samples at my cookery demonstrations; I use a cookie press and join the cookies with the filling below. In an airtight jar they will keep for weeks. You can modify this recipe by adding 2 tablespoons of ginger or cocoa for a different cookie.

SHORTBREAD CREAMS

INGREDIENTS

125g BUTTER
250g LOLA'S ALL-PURPOSE FLOUR (PAGE 10)
1 EGG
100g CASTER SUGAR
2 tsp VANILLA ESSENCE

PREPARATION

Preheat the oven to 160°C.
Combine all the ingredients in a food processor.
Roll into small balls and press onto baking trays with a fork
or use a cookie press to form shapes.
Bake for 20 minutes on baking paper covered trays.
When cold, join with filling.

FILLING

200g PURE ICING SUGAR
2 tsp RASPBERRY JAM
2 tsp BOILING WATER

Heat the jam and water and sift in the icing sugar.

This slice cuts well if left to stand in the refrigerator overnight.

DATE SLICE

INGREDIENTS

PASTRY
1 tbsp GELATINE
1 EGG
100g BUTTER
60mL COLD WATER
40g PURE ICING SUGAR
300g LOLA'S ALL-PURPOSE FLOUR (PAGE 10)

FILLING
200g DATES
1 tbsp BROWN SUGAR
1 tbsp WATER
1 tbsp GOLDEN SYRUP
1 tsp MIXED SPICE

PREPARATION

Preheat the oven to 180°C.
Select a shallow 20cm square ungreased cake tin.

MIXING PASTRY

Soak the gelatine in 60mL cold water, then heat gently until dissolved. Cool.
Combine all the remaining pastry ingredients in a food processor or chop the butter into small pieces and mix the ingredients together by hand to form a firm pastry.
Divide the pastry and press half the mixture into the tin using your fingers.
Roll out the other half of the pastry between two sheets of plastic for the top of the slice.

MIXING THE FILLING

Warm the dates slightly in a microwave or over a saucepan of hot water.
Combine the remainder of the filling ingredients with the softened dates in a food processor or beat with a wooden spoon. Spread the filling onto the pastry base in the tin and place the rolled out pastry on the top of the date mixture. Prick the top to allow air to escape and give an even appearance when cooked. Brush with water and sprinkle with sugar.

BAKING

Place in the oven and cook for 20 minutes. Cool in the cake tin and cut into squares to serve.
Note: The slice can be topped with a lemon icing if desired.

LEMON ICING

120g SIFTED PURE ICING SUGAR
1 tsp MELTED BUTTER
LEMON JUICE TO MIX
1 tbsp BOILING WATER

Combine all ingredients to make a creamy icing and pour onto the slice.

CHRISTMAS COOKIES

INGREDIENTS

65mL OLIVE OIL
2 tbsp TREACLE
300g LOLA'S BREAD AND PASTRY FLOUR (PAGE 11)
100g CASTER SUGAR
2 tbsp GROUND GINGER
1 tbsp MIXED SPICE
1 EGG, LIGHTLY BEATEN

PREPARATION

Preheat the oven to 150°C.
Cover a tray with baking paper.

MIXING

Place the oil and treacle in a saucepan and gently warm.
Remove from the heat and add three-quarters of the flour and the remaining ingredients. Mix well with a wooden spoon.
Tip onto a plastic sheet or board and knead the remaining flour into the pastry. Roll out between two sheets of plastic. Cut out in desired shapes and place on the covered tray.

BAKING

Place on the centre shelf in your oven and bake for 10 minutes until just firm to touch. Cool on the tray.

DECORATING

White chocolate can be used to dip the tops of cookies. Decorate with sprinkles.
Fill star centres with crushed boiled lollies.

FLORENTINES

INGREDIENTS

80mL OLIVE OIL
3 tbsp RICE SYRUP
3 tbsp LIQUID GLUCOSE
3 tsp VANILLA ESSENCE
3 tsp ALMOND ESSENCE
1 tbsp WATER
100g LOLA'S ALL-PURPOSE FLOUR (PAGE 10)
100g SUGAR
1 tsp GLUTEN-FREE BAKING POWDER
25g BABY RICE CEREAL
25g ALMOND MEAL
25g FLAKED ALMONDS
200g CHOCOLATE FOR COATING

PREPARATION

Preheat the oven to 200°C.
Line an oven tray with baking paper.

MIXING

Place the oil, rice syrup, liquid glucose, vanilla and almond essence, and water in a large saucepan and bring to the boil.

Combine the dry ingredients in a large bowl and mix to combine. When the liquid is boiling and frothy, remove from the heat and tip the dry ingredients into the saucepan. Stir well.

BAKING

Place teaspoonfuls of the mixture onto the baking paper in small mounds, leaving room for the mixture to spread to about three times its size.

Reduce the heat of the oven to 150°C and place the cookies in the oven for 5 minutes.

Open the oven door and press the cookies flat with a fork. Continue cooking for an additional 10 minutes until they are golden and quite flat. Flatten again if they rise too much; they need to be flattened to make them crisp.

Remove from the oven and cool on the tray.

Coat one side with melted chocolate scraped on with a fork.

This polenta porridge is quick and easy to make and children really love it with yoghurt and brown sugar. For added nutrition, throw in a few sultanas and serve with sliced banana. The recipe is for a single serve.

HOLLY'S YELLOW PORRIDGE

INGREDIENTS

1 cup BOILING WATER
¼ cup FINE POLENTA
¼ tsp SALT
1 tbsp SUGAR
¼ cup MILK

PREPARATION

Place the boiling water in a saucepan on high heat and boil rapidly.
While briskly stirring the water with a wooden spoon, trickle the polenta into the saucepan in a fine steady stream.
Continue, stirring, until it is thick and cooked (about 2 minutes).
Stir in the salt, sugar and milk, and serve hot with yoghurt and brown sugar.

PLAIN COOKIES

INGREDIENTS

4 EGG WHITES
150g CASTER SUGAR
100g BROWN SUGAR
2 tsp VANILLA ESSENCE
100g LOLA'S ALL-PURPOSE FLOUR (PAGE 10)
100g RICE FLOUR

PREPARATION

Preheat the oven to 150°C.
Cover a baking tray with greaseproof or baking paper.

MIXING

Place the egg whites, caster sugar, brown sugar and vanilla essence in a large bowl and hand whisk over a saucepan of hot water until the mixture is slightly warm and frothy. Remove from the heat and continue beating with a rotary or electric beater until the mixture is stiff; fold in the combined flours.

BAKING

Using a piping bag and large star pipe or a teaspoon, mound the mixture in little peaks onto the prepared oven tray, allowing one cookie space between each peak for expansion. Bake for 20 minutes and leave for a further 10 minutes to cook, with the oven door partly open. As this is a meringue mixture it takes a little longer to dry out. Let cool on the trays.

The plain cookies used for this recipe are topped with marshmallow, and covered with sprinkles or dipped in chocolate for a special treat. They can be iced and topped with sprinkles for fairy top cookies or be crushed and frozen for use as a baked cheesecake base. Tip: Freeze the marshmallow-topped cookies and dip into warm chocolate for delicious chocolate marshmallow cookies.

MARSHMALLOW

INGREDIENTS

$^1/_2$ cup WATER
$^1/_2$ cup SUGAR
2 tbsp GELATINE
2 tsp VANILLA ESSENCE
1 EGG WHITE

PREPARATION

Place the cold water, sugar and gelatine in a microwave bowl and stand for a few minutes to soften the gelatine.

Heat for 2 minutes in the microwave. Remove and whisk to dissolve any remaining sugar; add the vanilla essence.

Beat the egg white in a large mixer bowl and, while it is beating, slowly spoon in the gelatine mixture. Continue beating until stiff and fluffy.

Use as desired.

USES FOR MARSHMALLOW

Pipe or spoon onto the tops of plain cookies and top with sprinkles or coloured coconut.

Set in a slice pan, cut into squares and top with toasted coconut.

Use as a topping for slices or as a filling for sponge instead of cream for a lactose-free birthday cake. Set in a sponge tin, a spread of jam will join the marshmallow to the cakes.

Set in shallow patty pans and freeze for 15 minutes before dipping into chocolate coating and rolling in shredded coconut or crushed nuts.

MINI PIZZAS

INGREDIENTS

$\frac{1}{2}$ cup HOT WATER
1 tsp EACH GELATINE, SUGAR AND SALT
1 tbsp INSTANT DRY YEAST (FERMIPAN RECOMMENDED)
100g LOLA'S BREAD AND PASTRY FLOUR (PAGE 11)
2 tbsp ARROWROOT

PREPARATION

Preheat the oven to 200°C.

Mix all the ingredients together and cover. Let rest for 10 minutes, then mix again and pour a small quantity into greased flat-bottomed patty pans.

If you wish to freeze the bases, add 1 teaspoon olive oil to the mixture.

Place the topping on the raw pizzas before cooking for 10–15 minutes at 200°C.

If you prefer a 'crunchy' pastry, bake for 10 minutes and then add the topping and cook for a further 10 minutes.

TOPPING

GLUTEN-FREE PIZZA SAUCE OR PEELED CANNED TOMATOES
ONION SLICES
OLIVES
BACON PIECES
CAPSICUM
HERBS
CHEESE
Combine all the topping ingredients and spoon onto the uncooked bases.

PLAYDOUGH

INGREDIENTS

¾ cup WATER
FOOD COLOUR (CAREFULLY CHECK INGREDIENTS)
2 tbsp PSYLLIUM
2 tbsp BABY OIL
2 tbsp SALT
2 tbsp CITRIC ACID
1 cup POTATO FLOUR
1 cup RICE FLOUR

PREPARATION

Place the water and food colour in a small mixing bowl.
Add the psyllium and let stand for 5 minutes.
Stir in the oil and dry ingredients.
If sticky, add a little more oil.

Keep in a screw-top jar in the refrigerator.

SAVOURY SQUARES

INGREDIENTS

1 tbsp GELATINE
65mL WATER
65mL OLIVE OIL
100g LOLA'S BREAD AND PASTRY FLOUR (PAGE 11)
2 tbsp RICE FLOUR
1 tsp SALT
1 tsp BICARBONATE OF SODA
1 tbsp SESAME SEEDS

PREPARATION

Preheat the oven to 180°C.
You will need a large flat tray or one or more ceramic tiles to cook the squares.
Place the gelatine into the cold water and leave to soften; add it to the oil.

MIXING

Place the flour, rice flour, salt and bicarbonate of soda into a sieve.
Warm the oil and gelatine mixture in a saucepan and sift in the dry ingredients.
Mix the dough well until it forms a ball and will easily leave the sides of the saucepan.
Tip out and roll up in plastic and let cool slightly before use.

BAKING

Roll out thinly between two sheets of baking paper. Remove the top sheet.
Cut the pastry into squares with a pizza cutter or sharp knife and prick with a fork.
Brush with water and sprinkle with sesame seeds.
Lift the paper with the squares onto the tray or tiles in the oven.
Bake for about 10 minutes until the crackers are pale golden. Cool in the oven.

Do not use flour to roll out the crackers; use a smear of oil if necessary.

WHEAT-FREE ANZACS

INGREDIENTS

60g ROLLED RICE FLAKES
125mL BOILING WATER
65mL OLIVE OIL
200g SUGAR
2 tbsp GOLDEN SYRUP
150g LOLA'S ALL-PURPOSE FLOUR (PAGE 10)
1 tbsp MIXED SPICE
100g DESSICATED COCONUT
1 tsp BICARBONATE OF SODA

PREPARATION

Preheat the oven to 170°C.
Place the rolled rice flakes in a microwave bowl and pour the boiling water over them; leave for 5 minutes and then microwave on high in a covered bowl for 5 minutes.
Cover one or two large baking trays with baking paper.

MIXING

Add the oil, sugar and golden syrup to a medium-sized saucepan and warm gently for a few minutes (for a crisper cookie, bring to the boil).
Stir in the warm rice flakes, then add the flour, spice and coconut.
Finally, add the bicarbonate of soda dissolved in 1 tablespoon of boiling water; mix this stiff mixture well.

BAKING

Spoon onto the baking paper covered trays allowing room to spread and press down.
Bake for 15 minutes and cool on the trays.
For a less crisp result, reduce the oven temperature to 150°C.
Store in an airtight container.

DESSERTS AND WAFFLES

*This dessert can be made with canned or fresh
apple, but the rhubarb needs to be cooked
separately for the best result.*

APPLE AND RHUBARB CRUMBLE

INGREDIENTS

3 LARGE COOKING APPLES
$\frac{1}{2}$ cup SUGAR OR SUBSTITUTE
SMALL BUNCH RHUBARB

TOPPING

50g BUTTER
100g LOLA'S ALL-PURPOSE FLOUR (PAGE 10)
100g SUGAR
100g ALMOND MEAL

PREPARATION

Preheat the oven to 200°C.
Slice the cooking apples thinly and place in a greased pie dish.
Sprinkle with sugar or substitute.
Cut the rhubarb into small pieces and cook gently with sugar to taste.
Combine the topping ingredients.
Tip the cooked juicy rhubarb over the raw apple and sprinkle with the topping.
Bake for 20 minutes.

APRICOT CUSTARD FLAN

INGREDIENTS

FILLING
2 SAUCE BLOCKS (PAGE 8)
1 cup BOILING WATER
SUGAR TO TASTE
2 tsp VANILLA EXTRACT
1 tsp ALMOND ESSENCE
3 EGGS, LIGHTLY WHISKED
1 cup MILK
1 SMALL CAN APRICOT HALVES

PASTRY
1 tbsp GELATINE
60mL COLD WATER
300g LOLA'S ALL-PURPOSE FLOUR (PAGE 10)
40g PURE ICING SUGAR
NUTMEG FOR SPRINKLING
100g BUTTER
1 EGG

PREPARATION OF CUSTARD

Preheat the oven to 180°C.

Select a 20cm ungreased deep pie dish.

In a saucepan, add the sauce blocks to the boiling water and stir over a low heat until thickened.

Sweeten and add the vanilla and almond essences. Stir in the whisked eggs and milk.

MIXING PASTRY

Soak the gelatine in the cold water, then heat gently until dissolved. Cool.

Combine all the remaining pastry ingredients in a food processor or chop the butter into small pieces and mix the ingredients together by hand to form a firm pastry.

Press the the pastry into the pie dish with your fingers, making sure you have a thick cover.

ASSEMBLING THE FLAN

Arrange the apricots, curved sides up, around the pie dish and pour the custard over the top. Sprinkle with nutmeg and bake for 20–30 minutes.

Tip: The use of sauce blocks here will prevent curdling and cut the amount of milk necessary for this dessert. It can be made lactose-free by using all water.

APPLE SPONGE DESSERT

INGREDIENTS

4 LARGE COOKING APPLES
100g SUGAR
65mL COLD WATER
1 tbsp BUTTER
65mL HOT WATER
1 LARGE EGG
100g LOLA'S BREAD AND PASTRY FLOUR (PAGE 11)
60g CASTER SUGAR
1 tsp GLUTEN-FREE BAKING POWDER

PREPARATION

Peel, core and slice the apples.

Place in a microwave bowl or saucepan with the 100g of sugar and the cold water and cook until soft. Place the cooked apples into a greased ovenproof dish about 20cm in diameter.

Preheat the oven to 180°C.

MIXING

Place the butter in the hot water to melt.

Beat the egg and caster sugar together until thick and creamy.

Blend the flour and baking powder into the creamy egg mixture.

Add the cooled water and butter mixture to the bowl and stir to form a light batter.

Pour the batter onto the hot apple and place in the preheated oven for 10–15 minutes or until the batter is firm.

Serve warm with cream or ice cream.

Note: The batter mixture should be thin enough to pour easily onto the apples. As these flours often vary in consistency, it may be necessary to add a little more warm water to the mixture.

BAKED CHEESECAKE

INGREDIENTS

BASE
60g BUTTER
1 tbsp HONEY
120g CRUSHED WHEAT-FREE BISCUIT CRUMBS OR GLUTEN-FREE CORN CEREAL
40g DESICCATED COCONUT

PREPARATION

Melt the butter and honey over a low heat and mix with the cereal or crumbs. You may need a little hot water if the cereal is dry. Combine with the coconut and press into a loose-bottomed cake tin.

INGREDIENTS

FILLING
500g FIRM CREAM CHEESE
250g SOFT CREAM OR RICOTTA CHEESE
1 tbsp SOUR CREAM
200g CASTER SUGAR
2 EGGS
2 tbsp VANILLA ESSENCE
SPRINKLE OF NUTMEG

DECORATION

250mL CREAM
WHIPPED AND GRATED CHOCOLATE OR FRESH FRUIT

MIXING

Preheat the oven to 150ºC.
Beat the cream cheeses and sour cream with the caster sugar until creamy.
Add the eggs, one at a time, and whip on high speed.
Add the vanilla essence to the mixture and pour into the uncooked crumb case.
Sprinkle with nutmeg and place into the centre of the oven for 1 hour.
Turn the heat off and leave in the oven for an additional hour to set.
When cold, finish with whipped cream and fresh fruit or grated chocolate.

Don't worry if the cheesecake has a crack in the top, cream will cover it.

This recipe is used for the berry gate.. (pag. 5) and can be used to make a trifle or caramel ice cream cake using the creamy caramel sauce recipe (page 149) in the sauces chapter. It freezes well if foil-wrapped and so is a great standby. Cut in squares and serve filled with warm stewed apple to make a quick dessert.

CONTINENTAL SPONGE

INGREDIENTS

2 tsp MARGARINE
2 tbsp BOILING WATER
2 EGGS
75g CASTER SUGAR
80g LOLA'S ALL-PURPOSE FLOUR (PAGE 10)
2 tsp GLUTEN-FREE BAKING POWDER

PREPARATION

Preheat the oven to 180°C.
Place the margarine into a small bowl and add the boiling water; leave to melt.
Grease a 20cm flan tin and dust with flour or line it with baking paper.

MIXING

Whisk the eggs and caster sugar over hot water until they are just warm and bubbly.
Using an electric beater, beat until the mixture is thick and creamy but not stiff.
Fold the flour and baking powder into the egg mixture. Pour the water mixture down the inside of the bowl.
Turn the mixture with a wire whisk, being careful not to over-mix as this will release the air and flatten the sponge.
Pour into the tin and gently move the mixture with a spatula so that a small depression is made in the centre of the cake.

BAKING

Place in the centre of the oven and bake for 15 minutes. Stand for 5 minutes before turning out.
Tip: If the mixture will not pour from the bowl, it is too dry; add a little more warm water

CARAMELISED PEAR FLAN

INGREDIENTS

2 tbsp MARGARINE
$\frac{1}{4}$ cup BROWN SUGAR
1 LARGE PEAR, PEELED, QUARTERED AND SLICED INTO WEDGES
2 EGGS
$\frac{1}{3}$ cup CASTER SUGAR
70g BREAD AND PASTRY FLOUR (PAGE 11)
2 tsp GLUTEN-FREE BAKING POWDER

PREPARATION

Preheat the oven to 180°C.
Liberally grease a 20cm cake tin with the margarine, using all the margarine.
Sprinkle the brown sugar over the margarine.
Overlap the pear slices in the tin in a circular pattern.
Whisk the eggs and sugar until creamy, add the flour and baking powder, and pour over the pears.
Place the flan in the preheated oven and bake for 25 minutes.
Turn out immediately and serve warm with dairy-free custard.

DAIRY-FREE CUSTARD

INGREDIENTS

1 cup WATER
$\frac{1}{4}$ cup SUGAR
2 LOLA'S SAUCE BLOCKS (PAGE 8)
1 EGG, BEATEN
2 tsp VANILLA ESSENCE

PREPARATION

Bring the water and sugar to the boil, add the sauce blocks and let stand until blocks soften.
Return to the heat and whisk until the mixture thickens.
Add the beaten egg and vanilla.
Stir gently over the heat for 1 minute to cook the egg.
Do not let the custard boil.

CHRISTMAS PUDDING

INGREDIENTS

1 tsp NUTMEG
125g CURRANTS
150g SULTANAS
150g RAISINS
25g FINELY CHOPPED WALNUTS
25g SLIVERED ALMONDS
60mL RUM
125g BUTTER
125g BROWN SUGAR
1 tbsp GOLDEN SYRUP
150g LOLA'S ALL-PURPOSE FLOUR (PAGE 10)
50g ALMOND MEAL
1 tsp MIXED SPICE
1 tsp BICARBONATE OF SODA
2 EGGS
4 tbsp GLUTEN-FREE FLOUR FOR CLOTH

PREPARATION

Combine the fruit and nuts in a large mixing bowl; sprinkle with the rum. Cover and leave to stand overnight if possible. Before you begin to mix the pudding, half fill a large saucepan with water, place a saucer or rack in the bottom and, if you are using a pudding cloth, cut a 40cm square of calico. The cloth can also go into the saucepan. Place the lid on the saucepan and commence heating to boiling point. If using a basin, grease liberally with margarine or butter.

Note: There are two ways to boil a pudding depending on the size of the pot that you have. If you have a saucepan that is just large enough to take the pudding, water should not come more than halfway up the pudding. Keep the lid on the saucepan to prevent evaporation and watch the water level carefully, pouring more boiling water down the side of the saucepan; do not to pour it on the pudding. If you have a large boiler you can half fill it and when the water is boiling, plunge the pudding in and keep it rapidly boiling. Each method is successful, but the larger amount of water is less likely to evaporate and burn the pudding.

The recipe makes six to eight serves.
Please read these instructions before you begin.
The mixture may be boiled in a cloth, 45cm square of calico, or steamed in a pudding basin. Either way you will need a large saucepan or boiler to cook the pudding. Also, a saucer or rack in the bottom of the saucepan will prevent the pudding burning. To tie the pudding you will need some strong twine. As the pudding will freeze well it may be made months before Christmas.

MIXING THE PUDDING

Mix together the butter, brown sugar and golden syrup. Do not over-beat.

Add the flour, almond meal, spices and bicarbonate of soda to the fruit mixture.

Lightly beat the eggs and combine all the ingredients, turning with a large wooden spoon. The mixture should be quite firm to hold its shape; if not, add a little more flour.

COOKING IN A PUDDING BASIN: If you are using a pudding basin, grease the basin with margarine and spoon the mixture into the basin; cover with a loose piece of foil. Cook for 2 hours on the first day and heat up on the day of serving.

CLOTH METHOD: When the saucepan comes to the boil, remove the cloth with tongs and spread into a large strainer. Sprinkle the centre of the cloth liberally with the extra wheat-free flour, while the cloth is still hot. (This forms the skin of the pudding and so it is important to cover the cloth well with the flour.)

Make sure that the saucepan still has enough water in it and that it is boiling rapidly.

Spoon the mixture into the centre of the cloth and place a small piece of foil on top of the pudding so that it is just beneath the tie.

Tie the pudding with string, allowing a finger space between the tie and the mixture for swelling.

Leave a long strong loop on the pudding to hang it when it comes out of the pot. Boiling the pudding takes a little longer: 3 hours on the first day. Remove from the pot and hang to cool.

Boil up again for approximately 1 hour to remove from the cloth. This can be done on Christmas Day or a month before if you wish.

REHEATING

Cover the pudding with cling wrap and it may be reheated in a microwave. Use foil if you wish to reheat it in a low oven.

FLAMING

To flame the pudding in a traditional way it is necessary to first warm the spirit. Either brandy or whisky will flame well. Be careful if you are warming over an open flame as it will catch alight easily.

Mixed berries of any kind, fresh or canned,
are good for this spectacular dessert.
It makes a great adult birthday cake.

BERRY GATEAU

INGREDIENTS

1 CONTINENTAL SPONGE (PAGE 81)
1 PUNNET STRAWBERRIES
100g BLUEBERRIES OR 1 CAN MIXED BERRIES
100g SUGAR
100g RASPBERRY JAM
2 EGG WHITES
200g ICING SUGAR

ASSEMBLING THE GATEAU

When the sponge is cold, using a serrated knife, slice it carefully into three, commencing at the top.

Select about eight of the best strawberries from the punnet and set side.

Slice the remaining strawberries, add the blueberries and sauté with the sugar.

Spread the berry sauté mixture onto two layers.

If using canned berries, you will need to strain them and thicken the juice with a tablespoon of cornflour, then stir in the strained berries.

Stack up and coat the top of the sponge using a pastry brush and the berry jam that has been heated in the microwave.

MERINGUE COVER

Preheat the oven to 200°C.

Place the egg whites and icing sugar into a bowl and heat over hot water until the mixture is warm and shiny. Beat with an electric mixer until the mixture is stiff enough to pipe.

Decorate or spread the meringue to cover the cake.

Bake the meringue-covered gateau in the oven for about 15 minutes.

Finish with the selected strawberries dipped in berry jam.

Serve with berry coulis and yoghurt for a low cholesterol dessert.

WAFFLES

WAFFLES FOR BREAKFAST

INGREDIENTS

200mL MILK
150g LOLA'S ALL-PURPOSE FLOUR (PAGE 10)
1 tsp GLUTEN-FREE BAKING POWDER
1 tsp CHOPPED PARSLEY

65mL OLIVE OIL
PEPPER AND SALT TO TASTE
2 RASHERS BACON OR HAM
2 EGGS

MIXING

Brush the waffle iron with oil and heat according to the manufacturer's instructions.
Place the milk into a bowl and sift in the flour and baking powder and parsley.
Mix with a whisk to ensure a smooth batter. Add the oil, salt and pepper.
Remove the rind and chop the bacon or ham into small pieces; add to the batter.
Beat the eggs until light and fluffy and stir into the mixture.
The batter should be very thin so that it will quickly and easily cover the waffle iron.
Stir each time to distribute the bacon pieces. Cook according to the manufacturer's instructions.
Note: If the mixture is too thick, add a little water and whisk well.

WAFFLES FOR DESSERT

A non-plastic pastry brush is necessary to oil the waffle iron. Because the gluten-free flour is sticky, coat well with extra olive oil.

INGREDIENTS

2 EGGS
150g LOLA'S ALL-PURPOSE FLOUR (PAGE 10)
2 tsp GLUTEN-FREE BAKING POWDER

200mL MILK
2 tsp CASTER SUGAR
65mL OLIVE OIL

MIXING

Separate the eggs and beat the whites until stiff.
Combine the flour and baking powder and sift into the milk.
Add the sugar and oil, and whisk well to a smooth batter. Stir in the egg whites and continue to whisk until the batter is smooth.
Preheat the waffle iron and oil according to the manufacturer's instructions.
Cook each waffle for approximately 5 minutes.

LEMON DELICIOUS PUDDING

INGREDIENTS

2 tbsp MARGARINE
200g SUGAR
ZEST AND JUICE OF 2 LEMONS
4 EGGS, SEPARATED
3 tbsp LOLA'S BREAD AND PASTRY FLOUR (PAGE 11)
250mL MILK

PREPARATION

Preheat the oven to 180°C.
Grease a small casserole dish with margarine.

MIXING

Cream together the margarine, sugar, zest and egg yolks.
Add the sifted flours, milk and juice; stir to combine.
Separately beat the egg whites until stiff and fold into the mixture.

BAKING

Pour into the prepared casserole dish and place in the centre of the oven.
Cook for approximately 20–25 minutes until the sponge is firm to touch.
As there is custard underneath the sponge, the pudding will be a little wobbly when it is cooked. Serve warm with cream or ice cream.

This is a steamed pudding, so you will need a small pudding bowl. I have used a 13 x 6cm deep fluted metal jelly mould in the photograph. Select a saucepan that will fit the pudding basin. It is a light sponge pudding for three people and can be served with creamy custard or ice cream.

PLUM JAM PUDDING

INGREDIENTS

EXTRA MARGARINE TO GREASE THE BASIN
2 tbsp PLUM JAM
50g BUTTER
50g SUGAR
1 EGG
80g LOLA'S ALL-PURPOSE FLOUR (PAGE 10)
1 tsp GLUTEN-FREE BAKING POWDER
1 tbsp MILK

PREPARATION

Place the saucepan that will fit the pudding basin on to boil with enough water to come halfway up the pudding basin. Make sure that you have a tight fitting lid for the saucepan.
Grease the pudding basin well with some extra margarine, and cut a piece of greaseproof paper large enough to fit the top of the basin. The paper should be larger than the basin so that it will not let any water in when the pudding is steaming.
If you have a basin with a lid, do not use the lid for this recipe.
Place the plum jam in the bottom of the greased pudding basin.

MIXING

Cream the butter, sugar and egg together until fluffy.
Fold in the sifted flour and baking powder.
Stir in the milk and pour into the pudding basin.

STEAMING

Lower the pudding into the boiling water.
Loosely lay the greaseproof paper on top of the pudding.
Place the lid on the saucepan and keep the water boiling for about 40 minutes.
When cooked, turn the pudding out onto a plate to serve.

MAIN COURSE LUNCH AND DINNER

This is a meal in a soup bowl.

BEEF AND BEAN SOUP WITH DUMPLINGS

INGREDIENTS

500g GRAVY BEEF
3 LARGE POTATOES
3 LARGE ONIONS
2 cups THICK CARROT RINGS
1 CAN PEELED TOMATOES
1 cup DICED TURNIP
$\frac{1}{2}$ cup CELERY STICKS
2 OR 3 SAUCE BLOCKS (PAGE 8)
2 cups SHREDDED SPINACH LEAVES
1 LARGE CAN MIXED BEANS
SALT AND PEPPER TO TASTE

STEP 1

Cut the meat into large pieces and the potatoes into large chunks.
Add these along with the onions, carrots, tomatoes, turnip and celery to a large saucepan.
Cover with cold water and simmer for 2 hours.
After 1 hour add the dumplings to the boiling soup and continue boiling.

STEP 2

THE DUMPLINGS

1 tbsp PSYLLIUM
2 tbsp COLD WATER
1 EGG
1 tbsp OLIVE OIL
100g LOLA'S BREAD AND PASTRY FLOUR (PAGE 11)
2 tsp GLUTEN-FREE BAKING POWDER
$\frac{1}{2}$ tsp SALT

Sprinkle the psyllium on the cold water and leave for a few minutes to gel.
Whisk the egg and combine with the oil, flour, baking powder and salt; add the psyllium mix.
Spoon into the boiling soup and cook for 20–30 minutes.

STEP 3

Remove the dumplings and thicken the soup with one or two sauce blocks to your desired consistency; stir in the shredded spinach leaves and the canned beans and season with salt and pepper. Serve with dumplings.
Tip: Make sure that the soup continues to boil until the dumplings are cooked.

This is my dad's favourite. Make it the day before you need it and, like any casserole, the flavour develops, making this dish good for evening meals as it only needs reheating.

BRAISED STEAK AND ONIONS

INGREDIENTS

500g BLADE STEAK
100g POTATO FLOUR
2 tbsp OLIVE OIL
3 LARGE ONIONS, SLICED
2 cups COLD WATER
1 SAUCE BLOCK (PAGE 8)
SALT AND PEPPER TO TASTE

STEP 1

Preheat the oven to 160°C.
Cut the meat into serving-size portions and coat with a thin layer of potato flour.
Place the oil in a heavy pan and brown the meat well on each side.
Arrange in a deep casserole dish with a lid.
Add the onions to the pan and cook until brown and caramelised.
Pour the cold water over the onions and bring to the boil.
Add the sauce block and stir until a thick gravy.
Season with salt and pepper and pour over the steak.

STEP 2

Place the lid on the casserole and bake for 2 hours.
During the last hour place one serving each of a large piece of potato with the skin on in the hot oven.
Serve the braised steak with the oven-baked potato and fresh green beans.

For a lower cholesterol dish, the coconut milk can be replaced with one extra cup of water thickened with one sauce block (page 8) plus a few drops of coconut essence for flavour.

CURRIED CHICKEN THIGHS

INGREDIENTS

1kg SKINLESS CHICKEN THIGHS
50g LOLA'S BREAD AND PASTRY FLOUR (PAGE 11)
3 tbsp GLUTEN-FREE CURRY POWDER
2 tbsp BROWN SUGAR
2 tsp SALT
2 tbsp OLIVE OIL
2 LARGE ONIONS, SLICED
1 CAN WATER CHESTNUTS
1 GREEN APPLE, CHOPPED
1 cup COLD WATER
1 CAN LIGHT COCONUT MILK
2 tbsp SULTANAS

STEP 1

Remove any fat from the chicken thighs and halve if they are too large for serving.
Place the flour, curry powder, brown sugar and salt in a plastic bag and shake well to mix.
Add the chicken pieces to the bag and toss to coat the chicken.
Place the oil in a large pan and brown the chicken lightly to develop the flavour of the curry.

STEP 2

Arrange the chicken pieces in a deep ovenproof dish and cover with the onion, chestnuts and apple.
Add the cup of water to the pan and bring to the boil to deglaze the pan, extracting the flavour.
Pour the liquid over the chicken and vegetables; add the coconut milk and sultanas.
Cover the dish and microwave for 30 minutes or bake in oven for 1 hour at 180°C.

STEP 3

Serve with plain boiled rice and steamed green Chinese vegetables.

Read the instructions for assembling the pie before you commence, as it should be completed as quickly as possible while the pastry is warm. If it becomes cold, wrap it in a plastic bag and warm in the microwave for about 10 seconds.

FAMILY MEAT PIE

INGREDIENTS

250g CHUCK STEAK OR GRAVY BEEF
1 tbsp OLIVE OIL
1 ONION, CHOPPED
1 CARROT, GRATED
30g CELERY, CHOPPED
1 tsp SALT
2 tsp PEPPER
1 tbsp TOMATO PASTE
1 cup COLD WATER
2 OR 3 SAUCE BLOCKS (PAGE 8)
300g LOLA'S BASIC PASTRY (PAGE 132)

PREPARING THE FILLING

Chop the steak into small pieces and brown in the saucepan with the oil.
Add the chopped vegetables, salt and pepper and tomato paste; cover with the water.
Bring to the boil and simmer for about 1 hour until the meat is tender.
Remove from the heat and add the sauce blocks. When the blocks have softened, return to the heat and stir with a wooden spoon until the mixture is thick.

ASSEMBLING THE PIE

Preheat the oven to 200°C.
Make up the pastry and leave in a plastic bag to prevent drying until you are ready.
While the pastry is warm, divide into two, one piece slightly larger to fit the bottom of the pie tin. Roll out a large half between two sheets of plastic, then remove the top plastic and, using the bottom sheet to lift the pastry, flip it into the pie tin, plastic sheet up. Press in place through the plastic sheet leaving enough pastry to form the edge of the pie. Don't worry if it breaks a little as you can easily press it back together.
Pour the thickened pie meat into the uncooked pastry case. Brush the pie edge with cold water before adding the lid.
Roll out the top of the pie between the plastic sheets and slash the top to allow steam to escape.
Press with a fork to seal the edges of the pie. Glaze with egg wash (see page 122) or milk.
Place in the preheated oven and cook for about 25 minutes.
Serve as a main course with mashed potatoes and green vegetables.

This is a thick soup-like stew that is great for lunches as it is easy to carry to work in a thermos or can be quickly heated in the microwave.

HUNGARIAN GOULASH

STEP 1

To a large saucepan add 1kg veal pieces and a few bacon bones or a pork knuckle, and a few bay leaves.

Cover with cold water and boil for about 2 hours until the meat is tender. If possible, leave overnight to develop the flavour; remove the bay leaves and any fat and the bones.

STEP 2

3 LARGE POTATOES
12 SMALL ONIONS
2 cups THICK CARROT RINGS
1 cup DICED TURNIP
1 cup PARSNIP SLICES
SALT, PEPPER AND PAPRIKA TO TASTE
2 OR 3 SAUCE BLOCKS (PAGE 8)

Roughly cut the potatoes into large chunks; peel the onions and leave whole.

Add these with the other vegetables to the meat and stock.

Simmer on a low heat for about another hour until the vegetables are soft. Season.

Thicken with one or two sauce blocks to your desired consistency.

Tip: Freeze in individual serves for work lunches or serve with a fresh loaf of potato bread for a special lunch for all the family.

Sauce blocks used in this recipe will prevent the mixture curdling and give a firm texture when serving.

MOUSSAKA

INGREDIENTS

2 LARGE OR 4 SMALL EGGPLANTS
SALT AND PEPPER TO TASTE
500g MINCED LAMB
2 CLOVES GARLIC, CRUSHED
2 FINELY CHOPPED ONIONS
$\frac{1}{4}$ cup OLIVE OIL
1 TIN PEELED TOMATOES

$\frac{1}{2}$ cup MIXED CHOPPED GREEN HERBS:
OREGANO, BASIL, THYME AND PARSLEY
$\frac{1}{2}$ cup COLD WATER
2 cups MILK
3 SAUCE BLOCKS (PAGE 8)
3 EGGS, LIGHTLY WHISKED
50g GRATED MOZZARELLA CHEESE

STEP 1

Slice the eggplants in thick slices, sprinkle with salt and set aside.
Combine the lamb, garlic, onion, salt and pepper.
Use 1 tablespoon of the oil to grease a heavy pan to brown the meat without stirring, until it smells like barbecued lamb. Turn once and brown again for a few minutes. Add the tomatoes, herbs and cold water. Place in a saucepan and simmer for 15 minutes to distribute the herb flavours through the meat.

STEP 2

Rinse the salt from the eggplants with cold water and dry with paper towel.
Place the remainder of the oil in a large frying pan and lightly sauté the slices to enhance the flavour.
Set aside on draining paper to remove any oil.

STEP 3

Preheat the oven to 160°C.
Heat the milk in a saucepan until boiling, add the sauce blocks and whisk to form a thin sauce.
Add the whisked eggs to the custard.

ASSEMBLING THE MOUSSAKA

Use a large ovenproof casserole dish to bake your moussaka.
Pour a thin layer of custard in the bottom of the dish.
Arrange a layer of eggplant slices on the custard, then a thick layer of the lamb mixture.
Continue to layer the eggplant and meat until it is all used.
Pour the custard over the casserole and finish with the mozzarella cheese.
Bake for 1 hour, then turn the heat off and leave in the oven until set (about another half hour).
Serve with a green salad for lunch or dinner for all to enjoy.

This recipe came from my mother-in law, Kate Workman. Simply made, this casserole is a really economical meal for all the family.

LAMB CASSEROLE

INGREDIENTS

1kg BEST NECK OR FOREQUARTER LAMB CHOPS
50g LOLA'S BREAD AND PASTRY FLOUR (PAGE 11)
SALT AND PEPPER
2 tbsp OLIVE OIL
2 OR 3 CARROTS, QUARTERED
3 ONIONS, CUT IN RINGS
1 CAN PEELED TOMATOES
2 POTATOES, SLICED
1 cup COLD WATER
2 SAUCE BLOCKS (PAGE 8)

STEP 1

Preheat the oven to 180°C.
Trim all excess fat from the lamb chops and toss them in a plastic bag with the flour, salt and pepper. Brown the flour-coated chops well in the oil and arrange in a covered casserole dish.
Surround the chops with the carrots and onions and add the tomatoes and potato slices.

STEP 2

Pour the water into the frying pan to deglaze the pan; bring to the boil and add the sauce blocks. Whisk to form a thin gravy. Pour the gravy over the casserole. Cover and cook for $1\frac{1}{2}$ hours. Leave to stand for another half hour in the warm oven or until ready to serve.

Tip: This dish can be cooked 1–2 days before you need it, and the casserole does freeze well.

FETTUCCINI MARINARA

INGREDIENTS

1 BATCH OF GLUTEN-FREE FETTUCCINI PASTA (PAGE 20)
MUSSELS IN SHELL (1 EACH)
2 FILLETS WHITE FISH, APPROXIMATELY 200g, CUT INTO PIECES
100g PRAWNS
100g SCALLOPS
2 cups COLD WATER
3 SAUCE BLOCKS (PAGE 8)
SMALL BUNCH SCHALLOTS, CHOPPED
1 STICK CELERY, DICED
SALT AND PAPRIKA TO TASTE
FEW SPRIGS OF DILL (OPTIONAL)

STEP 1

Cook the pasta as directed on page 16 and place in a large serving dish.
Scrub the mussel shells and toss them for a few minutes in a pan to open.

STEP 2

Place the white fish, prawns and scallops in a saucepan with the cold water and bring
to simmer point. Turn off the heat and let stand for a few minutes to finish cooking.
Remove the seafood and set aside.
Add the sauce blocks to the hot fish stock and, when melted, return the mixture to the heat
and stir until thickened; stir in the vegetables and add seasoning and some dill if desired.

STEP 3

Combine the fish, scallops, prawns and mussels with the sauce and pour over the
pasta. When ready to serve, cover the dish and warm for a few minutes in the oven.

Tip: Always add the sauce to the pasta; don't try to add the gluten-free fettuccini to
the sauce, as it is too fragile.

SPANISH SEAFOOD BAKE

INGREDIENTS

250g WHITE BONELESS FISH
100g PRAWNS
3–4 SAUCE BLOCKS (PAGE 8)
SALT AND PEPPER AS DESIRED
$^1/_2$ cup DICED CELERY
1 LARGE ONION, DICED

SPANISH RICE TOPPING

1 cup RICE COOKED IN 2 cups COLD WATER
1 CAN PEELED TOMATOES
1 tbsp SUGAR
1 tbsp GLUTEN-FREE CURRY POWDER

STEP 1

Place the fish and prawns in a large saucepan and cover with cold water; bring to the boil and simmer for 5 minutes. Strain the fish and retain the stock to make the sauce.

STEP 2

Thicken the stock with the sauce blocks to make a thick sauce; season as desired.
Add the celery, onion, fish and prawns to the sauce. Spoon the fish into a casserole dish and top with the Spanish rice.

STEP 3

Place the rice in a large microwave bowl with the cold water.
Microwave on high for 10 minutes and let stand for 10 minutes until the rice is tender and the water has evaporated. Stir with a fork to check.
Mash the canned tomatoes and reduce by cooking over a low heat with the sugar and curry powder for about 5 minutes. Add this mixture to the cooked rice.
Stir through the rice and pile on top of the seafood mixture.
Finish with 2 tablespoons melted margarine combined with $^1/_4$ cup rice crumbs.

Serve with a green salad as a luncheon dish or with vegetables for an evening meal.

SUET-CRUSTED STEAK AND MUSHROOM PIE

INGREDIENTS

PIE FILLING
500g GRAVY BEEF
2 tbsp LOLA'S BREAD AND
   PASTRY FLOUR (PAGE 11)
2 tbsp OLIVE OIL
1 ONION
100g FRESH MUSHROOMS
1 tsp EACH SALT AND PEPPER
1 cup COLD WATER

PASTRY INGREDIENTS
$\frac{1}{2}$ cup COLD WATER
140g FINELY CHOPPED SUET
1 tsp SALT
330g LOLA'S BREAD AND PASTRY FLOUR (PAGE 11)

STEP 1

Chop the beef into bite-sized pieces and coat with flour. Place 1 tablespoon olive oil in saucepan and brown the meat well. Add the onion, mushrooms, salt, pepper and water and simmer with the lid on for 1 hour.

STEP 2
THE PASTRY

Add the cold water to a mixing bowl, stir in the chopped suet, salt and flour and blend with a knife until combined. Turn onto a board and knead for a few minutes. (This can be done in a food processor.) Divide the pastry to line the basin, leaving enough to form a lid to cover the filling. Roll out between two sheets of plastic and press into basin, making sure that the pastry comes over the edge to form a seal. Suet pastry should be thick as it is quite 'spongy' and light when cooked.

STEP 3
ASSEMBLING
AND COOKING

Add the filling to the pastry-lined basin then brush the edge with water.
Top the pie with the pastry lid, press down the edges and loosely cover with greaseproof paper.
Place a wire rack in the bottom of the saucepan and quarter fill with boiling water.
Carefully lift the pudding into the saucepan and boil for 2 hours with the lid on.
Note: Watch the water level, adding more boiling water down the side of the saucepan if necessary.

ALTERNATIVE

The pastry can be cooked on top of the stew in a saucepan to form a crust, called a 'sea pie' or rolled into balls (dumplings) and cooked in the bubbling stew. The stew must be boiling before adding the crust. When cooking dumplings it is better to thicken the stew after the dumplings are cooked and removed.

This recipe will make three individual quiches, 12cm each, or one 20cm quiche which can be frozen uncooked and cooked frozen as required. This pastry is rich but crumbly. For an easier handling pasty use the basic pastry on page 132.

QUICHE LORRAINE

INGREDIENTS	THE PASTRY	THE FILLING
	80g BUTTER	2 LARGE RASHERS LEAN CHOPPED BACC
	160g LOLA'S BREAD AND PASTRY FLOUR (PAGE 11)	60g GRATED TASTY CHEESE
	1 tbsp PSYLLIUM	4 EGGS
	1 tsp LEMON JUICE	1 cup MILK
		SALT AND PEPPER
		$\frac{1}{2}$ cup BASIC SAUCE (PAGE 148)

STEP 1

Blend the pastry ingredients together, add a little water if necessary to form a soft dough, and press into the quiche dish using a small sheet of plastic to prevent the dough sticking to your fing Chill in the refrigerator for a few minutes before adding the filling.

STEP 2

Sprinkle the chopped uncooked bacon and cheese over the base of the uncooked pastry base. Lightly whisk the eggs and milk with the salt and pepper, add the basic sauce and pour over the cheese and bacon (basic sauce here prevents the quiche from curdling if your oven is too ho Place the uncooked quiche onto a flat tray and freeze for at least an hour or until required. This can be done a day before if necessary.

STEP 3

Place the frozen quiche in a low oven of approximately 160°C for 25 minutes or until firm to touch on the outside of the top.
Turn the heat off and leave to stand for a few more minutes until the centre is set; it is important to overcook the filling.
Serve hot with salad or coleslaw.

Tip: For a dairy-free quiche, replace the milk with an additional cup of my basic sauce using sauc blocks and water (see page 8). Cheese can be replaced by corn niblets and the pastry made wit the basic pastry recipe (page 32).

*This is a traditional dish from South Africa.
I was introduced to this recipe when we hosted a Rotary student from
South Africa and I was asked to make this dish as part of a gala dinner. It
was so successful we adopted it as an entrée for our function centre.
Served with salad it makes a wonderful luncheon or a light main meal dish.*

BOBOTIE

INGREDIENTS

2 tbsp GLUTEN-FREE BREAD OR RICE CRUMBS
2 cups MILK
2 tbsp OLIVE OIL
500g MINCED LAMB
1 LARGE ONION, CHOPPED
2 tbsp GLUTEN-FREE CURRY POWDER
100g CHOPPED DRIED APRICOTS
2 tbsp SULTANAS
1 tbsp SLICED ALMONDS
SALT AND PEPPER TO TASTE
1 tbsp APRICOT JAM
4 LEMON OR BAY LEAVES
2 EGGS

STEP 1

Preheat the oven to 200°C.
Soak the bread or rice crumbs in $1/2$ cup warmed milk while you prepare the meat.
Place the oil in a heavy pan and brown the meat well with the onion and curry powder.
Add the soaked crumbs, apricots, sultanas, almonds, salt, pepper and apricot jam to the browned meat.
Spoon into a casserole dish and press the lemon leaves on top of the meat. Cover with foil and bake for 45 minutes.

STEP 2

Whisk together the remaining milk with the two eggs.
Take the meat from the oven and remove the lemon leaves.
Pour the egg mixture on top of the meat and return to the oven.
Reduce the oven temperature to 160°C.
Bake for a further 10–15 minutes to set the topping.
Serve at once with chutney, coconut rice and green salad.

MUFFINS, SCONES AND PANCAKES

With the brown sugar and ground almonds these muffins are not light and fluffy but are great for a nutritious breakfast. They freeze well in a plastic container.

APRICOT AND ALMOND MUFFINS

INGREDIENTS

1 tbsp GELATINE
2 tbsp PSYLLIUM
200mL COLD WATER
100g CHOPPED DRIED APRICOTS
150g LOLA'S ALL-PURPOSE FLOUR (PAGE 10)
2 EGGS
50g BROWN SUGAR
125mL OLIVE OIL
1 tsp VANILLA ESSENCE
1 tsp ALMOND ESSENCE
1 tbsp GLUTEN-FREE BAKING POWDER
50g GROUND ALMONDS

PREPARATION

Preheat the oven to 180°C.
Grease the muffin pans or line the pans with muffin papers.
Sprinkle the gelatine and psyllium on the cold water and let stand for a few minutes.
Chop the dried apricots in small pieces and sprinkle with a little flour to separate.

MIXING

Beat the eggs and sugar in a large bowl until thick and creamy.
Add the gelatine and psyllium mixture.
Stir the oil and essences into the mixture, then the flour and baking powder.
Fold in the chopped apricots and ground almonds.

BAKING

Spoon into the pans and bake for 20–25 minutes, depending on the size of the muffin pans.

CHOCOLATE CHIP MUFFINS

INGREDIENTS

250g SWEET POTATO
90g GOLDEN SYRUP
50g GLUTEN-FREE CHOCOLATE BUTTONS
$\frac{1}{4}$ cup OLIVE OIL
1 EGG
100g SUGAR
50g COCOA
2 tsp GLUTEN-FREE BAKING POWDER
$\frac{1}{2}$ tsp BICARBONATE OF SODA
150g LOLA'S ALL-PURPOSE FLOUR (PAGE 10)

PREPARATION

Peel and cook the sweet potatoes; mash in the saucepan.
Preheat the oven to 180°C.
Grease or use muffin papers in the muffin pans.

MIXING

Add the golden syrup, chocolate buttons and olive oil to the mashed sweet potato.
Beat the egg and sugar until thick and creamy.
Sift the cocoa, baking powder, bicarbonate of soda and flour carefully into the egg mixture.
Finally, add the cake batter to the sweet potato mixture and blend with a wire whisk.

BAKING

Spoon the mixture into the muffin pans; fill each pan almost to the top.
Let stand for 5 minutes before baking.
Bake for 15–20 minutes.

The crepes will freeze well but remember to thaw them at room temperature. They can be frozen in a bundle and will easily separate when warmed. They will heat quite successfully in the microwave on the lowest setting, covered. Serve folded with sugar and lemon wedges for a dessert, or with seafood sauce for a delicious lunch.

BASIC CREPES

INGREDIENTS

1 EGG
250mL MILK
100g LOLA'S ALL-PURPOSE FLOUR (PAGE 10)
1 tbsp OLIVE OIL
1 tbsp LEMON JUICE

MIXING

Beat the egg and half the milk together.
Add the sifted flour and the oil and beat until a smooth batter.
Thin with the remainder of the milk.
Let stand for a few minutes; adjust the consistency to a thin batter with additional water if required. Finally, add the lemon juice.
Leave to stand while you prepare the crepe pan.

PREPARING THE PAN

This important step will ensure even cooking of the crepes with any pan, even one with a non-stick surface.
Burn 1 teaspoon of butter in the pan.
Wipe out with kitchen paper and grease again with a small amount of butter.
Adjust the heat under the pan to a low temperature.

COOKING THE CREPES

Pour a very thin layer of batter into the pan and then tilt the pan quickly to give a good coverage. By the time the pan is covered the crepe should be set, if not the batter is too thick. To correct, add a little more water.
With a spatula carefully ease the crepe from the edge of the pan and flip it over to cook the other side for a few seconds.

Note: As each crepe is cooked, slide it onto a plate or piece of foil and cover with a cloth to prevent drying.

You will need some metal crumpet rings, a heavy frying pan or griddle and some extra oil to grease the pan and rings. Most good kitchen shops have crumpet rings or large egg rings; however, crumpets can be cooked in a waffle iron. If yeast is a problem, reasonable success is achieved with 2 tablespoons of baking powder to replace the yeast.

CRUMPETS

INGREDIENTS

1 cup WARM WATER
1 tsp SUGAR
1 tsp SALT
1 tbsp DRIED YEAST
1 tbsp PSYLLIUM
$\frac{1}{4}$ cup COLD WATER
1 tbsp OLIVE OIL
250g LOLA'S BREAD AND PASTRY FLOUR (PAGE 11)
3 tsp GLUTEN-FREE BAKING POWDER

PREPARATION

Place the warm water, sugar and salt in a bowl and stir in the yeast.
Let stand for about 5 minutes or until bubbles appear and the mixture is frothy.
In another bowl, add the psyllium to the cold water and let stand until it becomes a jelly.
Use a flat-bottomed dish or cake tin with about 1 cup of oil to grease the rings between cooking of the crumpets. Use a small pair of tongs to handle the hot rings.

MIXING

Combine the yeast and psyllium mixtures and add the olive oil and flour.
Finally, add the baking powder and beat well with an electric mixer to distribute the yeast; if the mixture is too thick to pour, add a little more warm water.

COOKING

Heat the pan and grease well; grease the rings and place in the pan.
Using a jug, pour in enough mixture to half fill the ring.
Cook on medium heat until the mixture starts to bubble and set.
Remove the ring and continue to cook on low heat until set; turn the crumpet. Lightly brown until the top is just coloured. You can use a lid to cover the cooking crumpets that will allow them to cook without turning.

STORING

Cool and pack in plastic wrap and refrigerate until ready to use.
The crumpets will keep for a week wrapped in the refrigerator.

SERVING

Toast and serve with honey.

CRUNCHY TOP MUFFINS

INGREDIENTS

100g MARGARINE
100g SUGAR
2 EGGS
1 tbsp VANILLA ESSENCE
1 tbsp GELATINE
1 tbsp PSYLLIUM
100g LOLA'S BREAD AND PASTRY FLOUR (PAGE 11)
3 tsp GLUTEN-FREE BAKING POWDER

TOPPING

1 tbsp RICE SYRUP
1 tbsp COCONUT
1 tsp MARGARINE
$\frac{1}{4}$ cup GLUTEN-FREE CORNFLAKES

PREPARATION

Preheat the oven to 200ºC.
Line a set of large muffin pans with papers.

MIXING

Place all the ingredients in a large bowl and beat until the mixture is light and fluffy (about 5 minutes on high speed).
Spoon the mixture into 6 muffin pans. Let stand for 5 minutes.
Combine topping ingredients and spoon on top of muffins.

BAKING

Place the cakes in the oven on a high shelf and cook for 15 minutes.
Remove from the oven and cool on a cake wire.
When cold, the muffins may be frozen in a plastic container such as an ice cream container or they may be wrapped in foil.
Note: Plastic wrap is not enough protection for cake in the freezer.

*These freeze well; separately wrap
and you can pop them in the toaster
frozen for a quick snack.*

DAIRY-FREE HOTCAKES

INGREDIENTS

EXTRA OIL TO GREASE PAN AND CRUMPET RINGS
2 EGGS
65mL LEMONADE OR SODA WATER
2 tsp VANILLA ESSENCE
2 tbsp OLIVE OIL
100g LOLA'S BREAD AND PASTRY FLOUR (PAGE 11)
30g CASTER SUGAR
2 tsp GLUTEN-FREE BAKING POWDER

PREPARATION

Measure and weigh the ingredients.
Grease a flat pan or skillet with a little olive oil.

MIXING

Separate the eggs and add the two yolks to a medium-sized mixing bowl,
retaining the whites to beat separately.
Add the lemonade, vanilla essence and oil to the egg yolks.
Combine the pastry flour, caster sugar and baking powder and whisk
into the liquids using a wire whisk. Set aside.
Whisk the two egg whites with a rotary or electric beater until stiff.
Stir the stiffened egg into the hotcake batter and whisk well.
Pour into a jug for easier handling while cooking.

COOKING

Place some of the extra oil in a small pie tin to oil the crumpet rings.
Heat the pan on medium heat.
Pour about half a cupful of batter into the greased pan.
Let cook until the batter is set.
Turn once to cook the other side.
Serve warm with honey or syrup.

DAMPER

INGREDIENTS

3 tbsp COLD WATER

1 tbsp PSYLLIUM

1 EGG

2 tsps MILK OR WATER FOR EGG WASH

1 tbsp GELATINE

1 tbsp GLUTEN-FREE BAKING POWDER

200g LOLA'S ALL-PURPOSE FLOUR (PAGE 10)

65mL WARM WATER

1 tsp SALT

PREPARATION

Preheat the oven to 220ºC.

Grease an oven slide or cover with baking paper.

Place the cold water in a bowl and add the psyllium.

EGG WASH

To make egg wash without using an additional egg: lightly whisk the egg in a small mixing bowl. Tip the egg into a large mixing bowl to use in the damper mixture, then add 2 teaspoons milk or water to the small bowl. Wash around the bowl with the pastry brush and you have egg wash to glaze the damper.

MIXING

Add the gelatine and baking powder to the flour and salt.

Add the psyllium to the egg and pour in the warm water, whisking lightly.

Sift three-quarters of the dry ingredients into the egg mixture and fold with a table knife to combine into a soft dough. Do not mix more than necessary.

Place the remaining dry ingredients on a board and tip the soft scone dough on them.

Knead very quickly a few times to combine all the ingredients.

Shape into a damper and mark sections with a knife.

BAKING

Place on the baking tray and glaze with the egg wash.

Cook on a high shelf in the preheated oven for about 15 minutes.

Remove from the oven and cool on a wire covered with a damp tea towel.

FAMILY PANCAKES

INGREDIENTS

3 EGGS
2 tbsp SUGAR
250mL MILK
150g LOLA'S BREAD AND PASTRY FLOUR (PAGE 11)
1 tsp GLUTEN-FREE BAKING POWDER
1 tsp CINNAMON
65mL OLIVE OIL
1 APPLE, FINELY GRATED

THE BATTER

Beat the eggs and sugar in a large bowl until fluffy, not dry and stiff.
Add the milk fold the flour, baking powder and cinnamon to the egg mixture.
Finally, add the oil and stir the grated apple into the batter and let it stand for a few minutes.

THE PAN

Brush a pancake pan with 1 teaspoon butter and heat until brown.
Wipe out the pan with paper towel and grease again.

COOKING THE PANCAKES

Pour about $\frac{1}{2}$ cup of batter into the hot pan and swirl the pan to cover the base with pancake batter. If it will not easily cover the pan, add a little water to thin the batter.
Cook for a few seconds on the other side.
Place the cooked pancakes in a stack and cover with a cloth or foil to prevent them drying.

SERVING

Serve warm, filled with stewed fruit such as rhubarb.

FLUFFY PIKELETS

INGREDIENTS

2 EGGS
2 tbsp OLIVE OIL
1 tsp VANILLA ESSENCE
65mL LEMONADE OR WARM WATER
100g LOLA'S ALL-PURPOSE FLOUR (PAGE 10)
2 LEVEL tsp GLUTEN-FREE BAKING POWDER
1 tbsp PSYLLIUM
25g MILK POWDER

THE BATTER

Separate the eggs, place the yolks in a large bowl and whites in a small bowl to be beaten later.
Add the olive oil, vanilla essence and lemonade or water to the yolks and whisk lightly.
Whisk the dry ingredients into the liquid mixture.
Beat the egg whites until firm and whisk into the batter.
Leave to stand as you prepare the pan.

PREPARING THE PAN

Season a small flat pan by first burning a teaspoon of butter in the pan, then wipe out with a paper towel. Melt another teaspoon of butter in the pan and heat. Pour out the surplus butter and the pan is ready to cook. If the pikelets are sticking, season the pan again.

Note: Even non-stick pans need to be seasoned to cook pikelets made with gluten-free flour. An electric frypan needs only a light oiling as the heat is regulated.

COOKING THE PIKELETS

Regulate the heat to low under the prepared pan.
Place a small amount of batter into the pan using a ladle or a small jug to pour the batter.
If the mixture is too thick to pour, add a little more warm water.
Cook the pikelet until it starts to bubble and looks firm on top.
Turn with a spatula and cook for just a few seconds on the other side.
Remove from the pan and keep covered with foil or a cloth until ready for use.

LOW-FAT DATE SCONES

INGREDIENTS

$\frac{1}{4}$ cup COLD WATER
1 tbsp PSYLLIUM
1 EGG
100g CHOPPED DATES
2 tbsp WARM WATER
250g LOLA'S BREAD AND PASTRY FLOUR (PAGE 11)
2 tsp GELATINE
2 tsp GLUTEN-FREE BAKING POWDER
2 tbsp PURE ICING SUGAR

PREPARATION

Place the cold water in a mixing bowl and sprinkle the psyllium on top.
Lightly whisk an egg in a small bowl, then add it to the psyllium mixture.
Add 2 teaspoons water to the small bowl and brush down with a pastry brush to make the egg wash to glaze your scones. (This makes an egg wash without using another egg.)
Preheat the oven to 200°C.
Cover a baking tray with a sheet of baking paper.

MIXING

Lightly whisk the egg and psyllium mixture and, using a knife to continue mixing, add the chopped dates and warm water, then the bread and pastry flour, gelatine, baking powder and icing sugar. Combine well with the knife and if still too sticky turn out onto a floured plastic sheet to knead in a little extra flour or fine rice flour.

BAKING

Cut out using a floured cutter, place on the prepared tray and bake for 10–15 minutes
Wrap in a tea towel to cool.

PLAIN SCONES

INGREDIENTS

$^1/_2$ cup COLD WATER
1 tbsp PSYLLIUM
1 EGG
2 tbsp WARM WATER
25g BUTTER
250g LOLA'S BREAD AND PASTRY FLOUR (PAGE 11)
1 tbsp GLUTEN-FREE BAKING POWDER
100g ARROWROOT
2 tsp GELATINE
2 tbsp PURE ICING SUGAR

PREPARATION

Place the cold water in a mixing bowl and sprinkle the psyllium on top.
Lightly whisk an egg in a small bowl, then add it to the psyllium mixture.
Add 2 teaspoons water to the small bowl and brush down with a pastry brush to make
the egg wash to glaze your scones. (This makes an egg wash without using another egg.)
Preheat the oven to 200°C.
Cover a baking tray with a sheet of baking paper.

MIXING

Lightly whisk the egg and psyllium mixture, then add the warm water and butter, using a knife.
Continue mixing, then add the remaining dry ingredients. Combine well with the knife and if
still too sticky turn out onto a floured plastic sheet to knead in a little extra flour or fine rice flour.

BAKING

Cut out using an oiled cutter and place on the prepared tray and bake for 10–15 minutes.
Wrap in a tea towel to cool.

PUMPKIN SCONES

INGREDIENTS

1 tbsp PSYLLIUM
$\frac{1}{4}$ cup COLD WATER
1 EGG
1 tbsp MILK FOR EGG WASH
125mL OLIVE OIL
1 tbsp HONEY
50g COOKED MASHED PUMPKIN
2 tbsp HOT WATER
300g LOLA'S ALL-PURPOSE FLOUR (PAGE 10)
30g MILK POWDER
1 tsp NUTMEG
2 tbsp GLUTEN-FREE BAKING POWDER
1 tsp SALT

PREPARATION

Preheat the oven to 220ºC.
Grease an oven slide or cover with baking paper.
Add the psyllium to the cold water and let stand to form a jelly.

EGG WASH

To make egg wash without using an additional egg, lightly whisk the egg in a small mixing bowl, then tip the egg into a large mixing bowl to use in the scone mixture. Then add 1 teaspoon milk to the small bowl, wash around the bowl with the pastry brush and you have egg wash to glaze the scones.

MIXING

Add the oil and honey to the mashed pumpkin and stir in the psyllium jelly, egg and hot water.
Place the flour, milk powder, nutmeg, baking powder and salt into the mixture and fold with a table knife to combine to a soft dough. Do not mix more than necessary.
Place a little extra flour on a piece of plastic, tip the soft scone dough on to it and knead through the plastic a few times.
Lightly oil your fingers and press out in a thick slab; cut into six thick scones.

BAKING

Place on the baking tray and glaze with the egg wash.
Bake on a high shelf in the preheated oven for 15–20 minutes.
Remove the scones from the oven and wrap in a damp tea towel to cool.

PERFECT PASTRIES

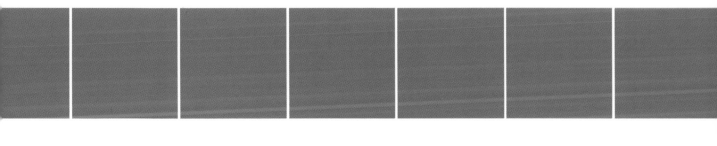

This pastry is free of dairy products, gluten, wheat and soy and sugar. There is no sugar in this recipe making it perfect for diabetics. In most cases the sweetener can be added to the filling, but if you wish you can add 2 tablespoons of pure icing sugar to the flour. This will make the pastry a little 'sticky' but is good for a slice base that requires little handling. The pastry does not shrink so can be used for blind-baked goods such as tarts filled with lemon butter (page 152).

BASIC PASTRY

INGREDIENTS

2 tbsp GELATINE
125mL COLD WATER
125mL OLIVE OIL
300g LOLA'S BREAD AND PASTRY FLOUR (PAGE 11)
1 tsp BICARBONATE OF SODA
1 tsp SALT
JUICE OF HALF A LEMON

PREPARATION

Sprinkle the gelatine on the cold water and leave to soften.

Place the gelatine mixture and oil in a large saucepan and heat to dissolve the gelatine.

Remove the oil mixture from the heat and sift in the dry ingredients.

Add enough lemon juice to form a soft dough.

Mix the dough until it forms a ball and will leave the sides of the saucepan.

Tip out on a plastic sheet and knead through the plastic, lifting and turning until the pastry is smooth. Allow to cool slightly before use.

Roll out between two sheets of plastic using a small amount of oil on your hands if necessary.

Note: This pastry is used in classes to introduce students to pastry making. It is quick and simple to make. It should be used warm; if it becomes too cold it will be difficult to handle but it is simple to warm in the microwave by first wrapping in plastic. Warm for about 15 seconds on high.

YELLOW PEACH STRUDEL

INGREDIENTS

4 LARGE YELLOW PEACHES, PEELED AND SLICED
$3/4$ CUP SUGAR

PASTRY
1 tbsp GELATINE
60mL COLD WATER
100g BUTTER
1 EGG
300g LOLA'S ALL PURPOSE FLOUR (PAGE 10)
40g PURE ICING SUGAR

PREPARATION

Preheat the oven to 180ºC.
Select a shallow 20cm square ungreased cake pan.

MIXING THE PASTRY

Soak the gelatine in 60mL cold water, then heat gently until dissolved. Cool.
Combine all the pastry ingredients with the gelatine mixture in a food processor or chop butter into small pieces and mix ingredients together by hand to form a firm pastry.
Divide the pastry and press half the mixture into the pan with your fingers.
Place the peeled and sliced peaches on the pastry base, then sprinkle with $1/2$ cup sugar.
Roll out the other half of the pastry between two sheets of plastic for the top of the strudel.
Cut pastry into strips and use to form a lattice over the fresh peach slices.
Glaze with the reserved egg white and sprinkle with remaining sugar.
Serve as a dessert or afternoon tea treat.

Tip: Peaches can be peeled easily if they are blanched in boiling water for a few minutes and then placed in cold water.

This mixture makes 24 cocktail crab quiches in 6cm pans. Make them in advance, freeze in the pans and cook frozen.

CRAB MINI QUICHE

INGREDIENTS

200g CAN CRAB MEAT

PASTRY
2 tsp GELATINE
3 tbsp COLD WATER
125g BUTTER
250g LOLA'S BREAD AND PASTRY FLOUR (PAGE 11)

CUSTARD
2 SAUCE BLOCKS (PAGE 8)
250mL BOILING WATER
4 EGGS, LIGHTLY WHISKED
250mL MILK
PEPPER AND SALT
CHOPPED CHIVES
PAPRIKA FOR SPRINKLING

MAKING THE PASTRY

Sprinkle the gelatine on the water and leave to stand for a few minutes; chop the butter into blocks and combine all the pastry ingredients to form a firm dough either by hand or in a food processor.
Cover the pastry while you mix the filling.

PREPARING THE CUSTARD

Add the sauce blocks to the boiling water and when they have melted whisk well. Add the eggs, milk, salt, pepper and chives. Place in a jug for pouring into the pans.
Do not add the crab meat to the custard; it is easier to place the shredded crab meat into the tiny uncooked pastry shell and pour the egg mixture into it.

ASSEMBLING AND BAKING

Tip: Grease the pans with a little margarine as the custard sometimes causes the pastry to stick.
Divide the pastry into four pieces for ease of handling.
Roll out between two sheets of plastic and cut circles with a cookie cutter to fit the pans.
Press each circle firmly into the bottom of the pans.
Place a small amount of crab meat in the uncooked pastry shell and pour the custard over it.
Sprinkle with paprika.
Freeze until ready to cook, or for at least 1 hour.
Preheat the oven to 160ºC.
Cook for 30 minutes until the custard is set.
Serve hot.

*This recipe makes four single serve pies
baked in 12cm tins.*

CURRIED CHICKEN PIES

INGREDIENTS

1 GREEN APPLE, CHOPPED
1 ONION, FINELY CHOPPED
1 tbsp OLIVE OIL
1 tbsp GLUTEN-FREE CURRY POWDER
1 tbsp BROWN SUGAR
SALT AND PEPPER TO TASTE
500g LEAN CHICKEN MEAT

1 tbsp POTATO FLOUR
250mL COCONUT MILK
2 SAUCE BLOCKS (PAGE 8)
1 SMALL CARROT, DICED
1 STICK CELERY, CHOPPED
300g LOLA'S BASIC PASTRY (PAGE 132)

**COOKING
THE FILLING**

Place the apple and onion in a pan with the oil.
Add the curry powder, brown sugar, salt and pepper.
Stir over a moderate heat for a few minutes to enhance the flavour of the curry.
Chop the chicken meat into large pieces and toss into a plastic bag with the potato flour; shake the bag to coat the meat with flour.
Reduce the heat of the curry mixture and add the chicken meat. Stir-fry for a few minutes.
Add the coconut milk and bring the mixture to the boil, stirring to prevent burning.
Remove from the heat and add the sauce blocks; let stand for a few minutes until the blocks have softened, then return to the heat and stir until the mixture is thick.
Add the carrot and celery and simmer for 15 minutes or cook in the microwave until the chicken meat is tender.

**COCONUT
MILK**

If you do not have canned or powdered coconut milk, you can make it by boiling 2 tablespoons desiccated coconut with 250mL of water; strain and use as coconut milk.
For a low cholesterol alternative, substitute with water and coconut essence.

**ASSEMBLING
THE PIES
USING
BASIC PASTRY**

Tip: Oil pastry thins as it cooks so don't roll it too thin and don't worry if it breaks as it will easily press back together. Do remember that it must be worked warm so prepare the filling before you start to mix the pastry.
Roll out half the pastry between two sheets of plastic to fit the pie tins.
Press into the tin, leaving enough pastry to form the edge of the pie. Roll out the top of the pies and slash the top to allow steam to escape.
Pour the thickened pie meat into the uncooked pastry case.
Using a spatula, dip the lid of the pie into a plate of cold water and slide it onto the meat to form the top of the pie.
Press with a fork to seal the edges of the pie. Glaze with egg wash or milk.
Place in the preheated oven and cook for about 25 minutes.

I used canned apricot halves, strawberries and kiwi fruit; the syrup from the apricots was used for the glaze. The pastry can be replaced by basic pastry (page 132) if you prefer.

PASTRY

65mL OLIVE OIL
2 tbsp LIQUID GLUCOSE OR RICE SYRUP
100g LOLA'S BREAD AND PASTRY FLOUR (PAGE 11)
20g BABY RICE CEREAL

Preheat the oven to 160°C.
Warm the olive oil and glucose and stir in the flour and rice cereal.
Tip onto a plastic sheet and knead lightly. Leave to cool.
Roll out between two sheets of plastic to fit six patty pans or one 20cm plate.
Bake the pastry for 15–20 minutes.

CRÉME PATISSERIE

50g BUTTER
3 tbsp LOLA'S BREAD AND PASTRY FLOUR (PAGE 11)
1 tsp ALMOND ESSENCE
2 tsp VANILLA ESSENCE
50g CASTER SUGAR
1 EGG
250mL MILK
125mL FULL CREAM

Cream the butter, flour, essences, sugar and egg together.
Heat the milk on a low heat to near boiling, but do not boil.
Tip the hot milk into the creamy mixture and whisk well to combine the ingredients.
Return the mixture to the heat and cook for a few minutes until thickened.
Remove the custard from the saucepan and set aside to cool.
Whip the cream and fold into the cooled custard.

ASSEMBLING THE FRUIT FLANS

1 SMALL CAN APRICOT HALVES
125mL APRICOT SYRUP
150g STRAWBERRIES
3 KIWI FRUIT

Fill the cooled pastry shells with créme patisserie, piling it high to support the fruit.
Arrange the fruit over the créme patisserie and glaze it with a pastry brush and warm glaze.

FRUIT GLAZE

Sprinkle 1 tablespoon of gelatine on top of 125mL canned fruit syrup and leave to stand until the gelatine is soft. Place the mixture into a microwave or stand in a bowl of hot water until the gelatine syrup is clear. Brush onto the fruit using a pastry brush.

FRUIT MINCE PIES

INGREDIENTS

FRUIT MINCE
500g MIXED DRIED FRUIT
1 GRATED APPLE
50g BROWN SUGAR
1 tbsp MARMALADE
1 tsp GROUND GINGER
1 tsp CINNAMON
1 tsp MIXED SPICE
125mL RED WINE OR SHERRY
125mL WATER
65mL RUM

PASTRY
1 tbsp GELATINE
65mL COLD WATER
65mL OLIVE OIL
1 tbsp LIQUID GLUCOSE
200g LOLA'S BREAD AND PASTRY FLOUR (PAGE 11)
1 tbsp LEMON JUICE

MAKING THE FRUIT MINCE

Simmer all the fruit mince ingredients together for approximately 1 hour.

Blend or chop slightly to combine all the ingredients. Fill glass jars and seal while hot if you wish to make the fruit mince in advance, or set aside while making the pastry.

MAKING THE PASTRY

Place the gelatine in the water to soften for a few minutes, then warm it gently until the mixture is clear. Add the olive oil and combine all the remaining ingredients in a food processor or mix by hand until you have a soft dough; add a little more water if the mixture is too stiff. Preheat the oven to 180ºC. Select and grease patty cake pans for the mince pies.

ASSEMBLING THE PIES

Divide the pastry into small sections as it is easier to handle.

Roll out between two sheets of plastic film, using a little oil to prevent sticking, and cut medium thickness with a scone cutter to fit the bottom of the tins; the pastry will thin as it cooks.

Press the pastry into the pans with the end of a wooden spoon, thinning it slightly.

Fill each pie with a teaspoon of fruit mix. Cut tops to fit the pies (I have used a star shaped cutter for the photograph). Dip each pie top into a saucer of cold water to seal the top.

Lift onto the filled pie with a spatula and press lightly around the edge of each pie with the point of a knife to make sure that the pie is sealed. Using a pastry brush, glaze each pie top with egg white and sprinkle with sugar. Bake for 20 minutes in the preheated oven.

JAM TARTS

INGREDIENTS

1 tbsp GELATINE
65mL COLD WATER
65mL OLIVE OIL
1 tbsp LIQUID GLUCOSE
100g LOLA'S BREAD AND PASTRY FLOUR (PAGE 11)
2 tbsp BABY RICE CEREAL
1/2 tsp BICARBONATE OF SODA
2 tbsp LEMON JUICE
YOUR FAVOURITE JAM

STEP 1

Select patty cake pans for the jam tarts. Preheat the oven to 150ºC.

Place the gelatine in the water to soften for a few minutes.

Heat the oil and glucose in a large saucepan until melted, not hot, and add the gelatine and the dry ingredients to the saucepan.

Stir in enough lemon juice to make a soft dough and mix well.

Roll out between two plastic sheets.

Cut the tart pastry with a fluted cutter and press into the ungreased pans.

Fill each with a small teaspoon of jam.

Bake for 15 minutes. (If the jam bubbles, the oven temperature is too high.)

COCONUT JAM TARTS

Make a coconut macaroon topping by beating 2 egg whites with half cup of caster sugar and adding 1 cup dessicated coconut. Spoon over the jam before baking.

CUSTARD TARTS

Sweeten some thick basic sauce (page 148) and add 2 or 3 whisked eggs to produce custard tarts; dust with nutmeg before baking.

APPLE CRUMBLE TARTS

Fill the pie shells with cooked apple. For the topping, use a mixture of equal parts almond meal, caster sugar, and gluten-free flour; rub in enough margarine until the mixture starts to become crumbling then sprinkle over the fruit.

MUSHROOMS

Make a few mushroom stalks by rolling some pastry in logs; bake the tart cases and the logs. Place a teaspoon of raspberry jam in the cooked tart shell, fill with whipped cream or mock cream, top with cinnamon and place the stem in position.

LEMON CHIFFON PIE

INGREDIENTS

PASTRY
60g BUTTER
120g LOLA'S ALL-PURPOSE FLOUR (PAGE 10)
1 tbsp PSYLLIUM
1 EGG YOLK (RETAIN WHITE FOR MERINGUE)
1 tbsp CASTER SUGAR
COLD WATER TO MIX

MERINGUE
WHITES OF 3 EGGS
100g CASTER SUGAR

FILLING
ZEST OF 1 LEMON
JUICE OF 2 LEMONS
250mL WATER
60g SUGAR
3 SAUCE BLOCKS (PAGE 8)
2 EGG YOLKS (RETAIN WHITES FOR MERINGUE)

STEP 1

Preheat the oven to 160°C.

Chop the butter into small pieces and combine all the remaining pastry ingredients to form a soft dough.

Knead for a few minutes, not using a food processor, to evenly distribute the butter.

Using a little rice flour to prevent your fingers sticking to the mixture, press into a pie plate. It does not have to be greased. Bake for 20 minutes.

STEP 2

Grate the zest of the lemon and squeeze the juice into the water; place in a saucepan with the sugar and heat to boiling point.

Add the sauce blocks and when melted whisk well.

Add the egg yolks and return the filling to the heat, stirring constantly. Stand the filling aside while you whisk the meringue. Do not pour into the pastry case yet!

MAKING THE MERINGUE

Beat the egg whites and the caster sugar to a thick meringue; add 1 tablespoon of the meringue mixture to the lemon filling. Fold through the mixture and pour it into the cooled pastry case.

Pile the remainder of the meringue onto the top of the pie and edges.

Return the pie to the oven and cook for a further 10 minutes until the meringue is set and lightly browned. Cool before cutting. Serve with pouring cream.

PARTY PIES

INGREDIENTS

FILLING

500g LEAN CHUCK STEAK
1 ONION, CHOPPED
1 tbsp GLUTEN-FREE SOY SAUCE
1 tsp SALT
2 tsp GROUND PEPPER
1 tbsp TOMATO PASTE
500mL COLD WATER
2 SAUCE BLOCKS (PAGE 8)

300G LOLA'S BASIC PASTRY (PAGE 132)
1 EGG WHITE TO GLAZE
PAPRIKA TO SPRINKLE

STEP 1

Mince or chop the beef finely and simmer with the onion, soy sauce, salt, pepper, tomato paste and water for 1 hour or until the meat is tender. Remove the meat from the heat and add the sauce blocks to the meat mixture; let stand until the blocks melt. Return to the heat and stir until the meat is thickened. Set aside to cool.

MAKING THE PIES

Preheat the oven to 200°C.

You will need a saucer of cold water, a pastry brush and a small knife, two sheets of plastic for rolling out the dough, a rolling pin, two circular scone cutters (one a little larger than the other), and a set of small patty tins.

Roll out the pastry between the sheets of plastic; it is easier to divide the mixture into smaller sections before you commence rolling.

Cut a larger circle to fit the pans and a smaller circle for the tops. Using a sharp knife, cut a cross in the top for an air vent.

Place a pastry round into the greased patty pan and press out to make sure that the pastry fits the pan.

Keep the pastry as thin as possible for a dainty party pie or a little thicker if they are to withstand a lunch box. Fill the pie with the cooled meat mixture.

Slide each pie top into the saucer of cold water, then lift with a spatula onto the pie. (The water will seal the edges of the pie.)

Press lightly around the edges with the point of a small knife to perfect the seal. Sprinkle with paprika. Brush the top of the pies with the egg white and cook for 15 minutes in the preheated oven.

It is important to keep this pastry warm for easy use; if it gets cold it will become crumbly and difficult to use. To reconstitute just roll it in the larger sheet of plastic and heat for 10–15 seconds in the microwave. Knead slightly through the plastic and it will be again pliable.

SAUSAGE ROLLS

INGREDIENTS

125mL COLD WATER
2 tbsp GELATINE
125mL OLIVE OIL
350g LOLA'S BREAD AND PASTRY FLOUR (PAGE 11)
1 tsp BICARBONATE OF SODA

1 tbsp PSYLLIUM
(soaked in extra $\frac{1}{4}$ cup cold water)
JUICE OF $\frac{1}{2}$ LEMON
500g GLUTEN-FREE SAUSAGE MINCE
EGG WASH FOR GLAZE (PAGE 128)
SESAME SEEDS FOR TOPPING

PREPARATION

Add the cold water to a saucepan and sprinkle the gelatine on top; set aside to soak for 1 minute. Preheat the oven to 180°C and place an oven shelf at the top of the oven. Cut a sheet of baking paper to cover the tray. Using scissors, cut the edges from plastic sleeves, open out to size of a double A4 sheet, then fold one sheet in half lengthwise to give you two long narrow strips of plastic.

MIXING THE PASTRY

Add the oil to the gelatine mix and heat until it comes to the boil, stirring with a wooden spoon to prevent the gelatine sticking. Stir in the flour, bicarbonate of soda and psyllium mixture; add enough lemon juice to combine the mixture. If the mix is a bit too sticky, add enough flour or rice flour to form a ball that will tip from the saucepan. Tip out onto the large plastic sheet and lightly knead.

PREPARATION

Divide your gluten-free sausage mince into four long sausage shaped pieces.
You will need a cup of cold water for sealing the rolls with your pastry brush.
Lightly whisk one egg for glaze. Have some seeds at hand if you wish to use them.

ASSEMBLY

Divide the pastry into four parts; use one part as follows, keeping the other three pieces rolled in the larger sheet of plastic to keep it warm. Using your hands, that have a small amount of oil on them, roll the pastry into a sausage about three quarters of the length of your long plastic sheets. Place the sausage shape between the two long pieces of plastic and gently roll the pastry to fit the long strips. Through the top plastic sheet, mark a straight edge with the back of a knife along each side of the strip. Remove the top sheet of plastic and any spare pieces of pastry. Place a roll of the mince evenly down the centre of the pastry, leaving enough pastry on either side to roll over. Using the underneath sheet of plastic, lift the top edge onto the mince. Peel back the plastic strip and brush the top of the roll with egg glaze, and sprinkle with seeds or paprika. Cut the roll into 12 pieces and place on the baking paper. Repeat the process. Warm the pastry in the microwave if it has become too cold to roll. Bake for 15 minutes. The sausage rolls freeze well.

SAUCES, STUFFING AND PICKLES

Use this sauce for pasta or vegetable dishes, or as a base for soups such as asparagus or fresh mushroom.

BASIC SAUCE

Two sauce blocks (page 8) will thicken 250mL of liquid for a thin sauce or soup base.
Use three blocks for a thick sauce.
Bring the liquid to the boil, add the frozen blocks and set aside until the blocks melt.
When the blocks have melted, whisk the mixture and return to the heat.
Stir until thickened.

CHEESE SAUCE – Add grated cheese.
CREAM SAUCE – Add milk powder, or sour cream or yoghurt.

CREAM SOUPS

Soups can be made with a water base and gluten-free stock cubes.

MUSHROOM CREAM SOUP

Add sautéed mushrooms to the basic sauce.

GREEN ASPARAGUS SOUP

Blend 1 can of green asparagus and juice with the basic sauce.

CAULIFLOUR SOUP

Blend cooked cauliflower with the basic sauce.
Use sauce blocks to suspend the vegetables in potato and leek or pumpkin soup.

This is an ideal sauce for chocolate ice cream cake using the continental sponge recipe (page 81) or for use with waffles (page 88).

CHOCOLATE SAUCE

INGREDIENTS
30g COCOA
125g BROWN SUGAR
125g BUTTER
1 tbsp GOLDEN SYRUP
1 TIN CONDENSED MILK
1 tsp VANILLA ESSENCE

PREPARATION

Sift the cocoa into a bowl with the brown sugar; melt the butter and gradually stir into the sugar and cocoa. Add the golden syrup and place the mixture in a saucepan over a low heat.
Stir constantly until the mixture forms a rich fudge mixture
Beat in the condensed milk with a wooden spoon and continue cooking for a few minutes until the sauce is smooth, being careful not to burn the mixture, then add vanilla essence.
Thin the mixture with a little warm water or brandy.

Serve warm in tiny individual ceramic pots with a platter of fresh fruit pieces, or poured over waffles, banana fritters or ice cream.

CREAMY CARAMEL SAUCE

INGREDIENTS

$1/2$ cup BUTTER
$1/2$ cup BROWN SUGAR
1 TIN CONDENSED MILK
1 tbsp GOLDEN SYRUP
3 tbsp BRANDY

PREPARATION

Melt the butter in a saucepan over low heat; stir in the brown sugar and cook for about 1 minute, until the mixture turns a light golden caramel colour.

Stir in the condensed milk and the golden syrup and cook for about 30 seconds over a very low heat.

Remove from the heat and stir in the brandy and enough water to thin to the consistency that you require.

GRANDMA'S TOMATO SAUCE

INGREDIENTS

3 CANS ITALIAN PEELED TOMATOES
250mL WHITE WINE VINEGAR
1 CLOVE GARLIC
150g SUGAR
$1/2$ tsp CAYENNE PEPPER
1 tsp ALLSPICE
1 tsp PEPPER
3 tsp SALT

PREPARATION

Boil the tomatoes and juice for 1 hour and then put the mixture through a strainer to remove any seeds.

Add the vinegar, crushed garlic, sugar and spices to the pulp and simmer for another hour or until the mixture is thickened.

Bottle and seal while hot.

Keep refrigerated.

GREEN PEPPER SAUCE

HOLLANDAISE

Serve with fish, smoked meats such as smoked turkey or hot baked ham or as a side dish with asparagus.

INGREDIENTS

250mL STOCK
2 SAUCE BLOCKS
1 tsp GREEN PEPPERCORNS
1 tbsp SOUR CREAM

PREPARATION

Heat the stock, then remove from the heat and add the sauce blocks. When they have softened, return to the heat and whisk into a smooth sauce.

Place the sauce, green peppercorns and sour cream into a blender and blend until smooth.

Leave to stand for at least 30 minutes for flavour to develop if possible.

Reheat to serve.

NOTE: If you have a china sauce boat, place the sauce in the boat and re-heat in the microwave at serving time.

INGREDIENTS

125mL WHITE WINE OR CIDER
    VINEGAR
1 SLICE OF ONION
2 BAY LEAVES
1 TEASPOON BLACK
    PEPPERCORNS
125g BUTTER
4 EGG YOLKS
JUICE OF 1 LEMON

STEP 1

Place the vinegar, onion, bay leaves and peppercorns in a saucepan and boil until the mixture reduces by about a third. Strain and set aside to cool.

Soften the butter, but do not melt it. This can be done successfully in a microwave on low temperature or simply leave it out of the refrigerator in warm weather.

STEP 2

Place the egg yolks into a metal basin and whisk in the vinegar mixture.

Whisk this mixture over a saucepan of hot water until it just begins to thicken.

Remove from the heat and whisk in about 1 tablespoon of the softened butter, using a wire whisk or an electric beater.

Continue beating, adding the butter a little at a time until the mixture is thick and creamy.

Beat in the lemon juice to taste.

Note: Hollandaise can be kept in the refrigerator, but should be served at room temperature.

HOME-MADE STOCK

ITALIAN PASTA SAUCE

Home-made stock can be used in this recipe instead of water and stock cubes.

This stock can be made from the baking dish juices or any time that you are pan frying meat, chicken or fish. Always keep the stock from baking or pan frying meat. Simply pour water into the pan, scrape the pan, bring to the boil and set aside to cool. Remove any solidified fat and freeze until you need some stock. Fish heads or fins can be boiled up for fish stock and bones bought from the butcher if you need extra stock. It is a good idea to freeze the stock in measured quantities, such as 1 cup portions, which can be easily removed from the freezer for use. Tea cups can be used and the blocks removed as soon as they are solid. Store the stock blocks in a plastic bag ready for use.

INGREDIENTS

2 RASHERS BACON
1 MEDIUM-SIZED ONION, SLICED
2 CLOVES GARLIC
425g CAN ITALIAN TOMATOES
1 GLUTEN-FREE STOCK CUBE
250mL HOT WATER
2 SAUCE BLOCKS (PAGE 8)
$\frac{1}{2}$ CAPSICUM, CHOPPED
$\frac{1}{2}$ CUP CHOPPED CELERY
100g GRATED MOZZARELLA
  CHEESE

MAKING THE SAUCE

Remove the rind from the bacon and chop the bacon into small pieces. Fry the bacon, onion and garlic together until browned.

Drain the tomatoes and set the juice aside. Chop the tomatoes into small pieces and add to the bacon and onion mixture.

Add the stock cube to the water and stir to dissolve the cube.

Pour the tomato juice into the stock and bring the liquid to the boil.

Add 2 sauce blocks and leave to stand until the blocks melt.

Return to the heat and stir until thickened.

Add the bacon, vegetables and cheese to the thickened sauce and serve with pasta.

*This is a delicious filling for tarts
or spread for pikelets.*

*Keep this mayonnaise in the refrigerator. To make a
lighter salad cream for coleslaw dressing, add 1
tablespoon water to the finished mayonnaise.*

LEMON BUTTER   MAYONNAISE

INGREDIENTS

4 EGGS
200g SUGAR
125g BUTTER, AT ROOM
   TEMPERATURE
JUICE AND ZEST OF 2 LEMONS

PREPARATION

Whisk the eggs and sugar together in a bowl and beat
in the lemon juice.

Place the bowl over a saucepan of simmering water
and whisk until the mixture has thickened.

Remove from the heat and beat in the softened butter,
a little at a time.

Return to the heat and whisk for 1 minute.

Bottle and seal in screwtop jars while hot.

Keep refrigerated and serve with pikelets or in tarts.

INGREDIENTS

4 EGG YOLKS
1 tbsp CASTER SUGAR
1 tsp SALT
1 tsp POWDERED MUSTARD
$\frac{1}{2}$ cup OLIVE OIL
1 tbsp WHITE WINE VINEGAR

PREPARATION

Using an electric blender, process the egg yolks, sugar,
salt and mustard for about 1 minute.

With the machine running, slowly pour in the oil, then add
the vinegar and beat until thick.

MUSHROOM PASTA SAUCE

PISTACHIO STUFFING

This delicious stuffing can be used in poultry, pork or veal. Wheat-free breadcrumbs may be used to replace some of the cooked rice.

INGREDIENTS

250g FRESH MUSHROOMS
1 tsp BUTTER
1 cup CHICKEN OR VEGETABLE
   STOCK
1 tsp DRIED ONION
2 SAUCE BLOCKS (PAGE 8)
GROUND PEPPER AND SALT

MAKING THE SAUCE

Chop or slice the mushrooms and sauté for a few minutes in a frying pan with a teaspoon of butter. Set aside.

Place the stock in a saucepan, add the onion and bring to the boil.

Remove from the heat and place the sauce blocks in the boiling stock to melt.

Whisk the mixture and return to the heat, stirring until thickened (about 1 minute).

Add the sautéed mushrooms to the sauce and season with the pepper and salt.

INGREDIENTS

130g COOKED RICE
75g CHOPPED BACON
1 SMALL ONION
1 level tsp FRESH THYME OR
MIXED HERBS
50g SHELLED PISTACHIO NUTS
SALT AND PEPPER TO TASTE

Combine all the ingredients and mix well.

SWEET MUSTARD PICKLES

INGREDIENTS

200g CAULIFLOWER PIECES
2 MEDIUM-SIZED CHOKOS
3 LARGE ONIONS
4 OR 5 GREEN TOMATOES
1 cup BROWN CIDER VINEGAR
375mL WHITE WINE VINEGAR
$^3/_4$ cup BROWN SUGAR
2 tbsp TURMERIC
1 tbsp DRIED MUSTARD
2 tbsp CORNFLOUR
2 tbsp POTATO FLOUR
1 tsp POWDERED GINGER

BRINE

$^1/_2$ CUP SALT
2 CUPS HOT WATER
Add the salt to the hot water and stir until dissolved.
Let cool slightly and pour over the vegetable

DAY 1

Cut the cauliflower into small pieces; slice or chop the other vegetables as you desire.
Cover with the brine and leave to stand overnight. If you like pickles chunky, then you can leave larger pieces. The total weight of the vegetables should be approximately 1kg.

DAY 2

Wash the brine from the vegetables under cold water.
Place the vinegars and sugar into a large saucepan and add the vegetables.
Bring to the boil and cook for approximately 20 minutes, until the vegetables are tender but still firm.
Mix together $^1/_2$ cup cold water with the turmeric, mustard, cornflour, potato flour and ginger to form a paste.
Thicken the vegetables by stirring the paste into the vegetables.
Cook for a few minutes until the mixture thickens and then pour into jars and seal immediately with screwtop lids. Turn upside down to cool.
Check the seal: the top should be concave when the pickle is cold; if not, remove the lid and heat again by placing the jar of pickles in a saucepan of water. Bring to the boil or place in a microwave for 1 minute. Seal again as before.

For use with chicken, fish or pork,
or on stir-fried vegetables

SWEET AND SOUR SAUCE

INGREDIENTS

1 x 450g CAN OF PINEAPPLE
  PIECES IN SYRUP
1 tbsp BROWN SUGAR
125mL WHITE WINE VINEGAR
1 tsp GRATED GREEN GINGER
100g MIXED SLICED RAW
  VEGETABLES: CARROT, CELERY,
  CAPSICUM, AND A FEW SLIVERS
  FRESH CHILLI)

PREPARATION

Drain the tin of pineapple pieces and use the syrup to make this sauce.

Place the syrup into a saucepan and add 1 tablespoon brown sugar and 125mL vinegar for each 250mL of pineapple syrup.

Heat the syrup over a low heat to boiling.

Mix 1 level tablespoon cornflour with a little cold water.

Remove the syrup from the heat and stir in the blended cornflour mixture.

Add the vegetables and green ginger and stir over a low heat for a few minutes to cook the sauce.

Note: If you prefer to use pineapple in natural juice, add extra brown sugar to the mixture.

VEGETABLE STUFFING

INGREDIENTS

1 cup CAULIFLOUR PIECES
1 cup GREEN BEANS, SLICED
$\frac{1}{2}$ cup GRATED MOZZARELLA
  CHEESE
SALT AND PEPPER TO TASTE
$\frac{1}{2}$ cup CHOPPED ONION
$\frac{1}{2}$ cup SLICED WATER CHESTNUTS

PREPARATION

Place the cauliflour and beans in a saucepan, cover with cold water and bring to the boil.

Drain the vegetables and add the cheese, salt and pepper, onion and the water chestnuts.

Use as desired to stuff veal or chicken.

TROUBLESHOOTING

Dear Lola,

My coeliac child now suffers from constipation and I am trying to include more fibre in his diet. I am using psyllium as you suggested in the bread but can I use this product in other recipes such as muffins?

Psyllium is easy to use in muffin recipes as 1 tablespoon of the fibre can be added to the flour. You may need to add a little more water depending on the recipe. For recipes such as scones I find it better to add the tablespoon of psyllium to a quarter cup of water and let it 'gel' for a few minutes before adding to the mixture; this way there is no guesswork.

Dear Lola,

I am trying to make baby rusks without eggs, can you help?

I have had success with egg replacer using my rusk recipe that is derived from my sandwich bread recipe, but more recently I found that egg replacer also works well with the potato bread recipe. This is good when you need bread rolls for school, but the potato makes it a little too soft and brittle for rusks.

Dear Lola,

I bought some besan flour from a health food shop to make your flour blend, but the besan flour was very bitter. Can I use some other flour?

Besan flour is not bitter to taste, even the cheaper brands that are imported from India are not bitter, but some have an earthy curry flavour. I think the flour you were sold as besan flour is yellow pea flour; this is a very bitter product. As good quality besan flour has increased in price, some shops are selling this cheaper flour as besan. The best brand of besan is the colour of custard powder and does not have black specs in it.

Dear Lola,

My bread recipe is working well except that it burns on top and this makes a hard crust, difficult to slice. I have tried foil but it still burns.

With fan ovens the heat still manages to lift the foil. I use a flat scone tray on top of the bread tin; this works well to give you a flat top as well as preventing the loaf from burning. Gluten-free flours are heat sensitive and do burn easily so try baking the bread on the lowest shelf and use an oven thermometer to check the temperature; if it is still burning reduce the temperature by 20°C.

Dear Lola,

Can you tell me which flour to use when I am making one of my husband's favourites, braised steak and onions? I have tried rice flour and cornflour but I don't like the gritty taste of rice flour or the aftertaste of cornflour.

If I am in a hurry and haven't any of my bread and pastry blend ready mixed, I use a thin coating of potato flour on the steak before browning; it thickens very well and makes a nice glossy gravy. Be careful not to use too much or you will get a gluggy mixture.

Dear Lola,

Is there an easy way to measure golden syrup when I am making cookies?
I love the flavour but it is so sticky I try and avoid these recipes.

There are a few easy methods of handling such products as golden syrup, treacle, rice syrup and liquid glucose. Many of these products are now packed in glass or plastic containers so that you can warm them in the microwave. If you are using oil in the recipe, use some of this to oil your measuring spoon and the syrup will then easily slide off. If you are weighing the product just oil the dish on your scales.

Dear Lola,

Why do you say to heat the eggs and sugar over hot water before beating in your sponge recipes? I usually separate the eggs and beat in the sugar.

Heating the eggs and sugar over a saucepan of hot water allows the mixture to be beaten without separating the eggs. Also, the warmed mixture whips in half the usual beating time, a great help if you only have a hand mixer. Separating the eggs and beating for a long time gives you a dry sponge that will not keep. My method can be used with icing sugar and egg whites to give a thick creamy meringue covering such as used in bombe Alaska. It sets in the oven in just a few minutes.

Dear Lola,

I thought rice was quite safe for coeliacs but in an Asian food shop I saw rice marked 'glutinous rice', can some rice contain 'gluten'?

Rice is quite safe for coeliacs and does not contain gluten. Glutinous rice is another name for 'sticky rice', a type of rice naturally containing rice syrup or sugar. It is generally used for making sweets such as baked rice pudding or sweet rice balls.

LOLA'S GLOSSARY

ALLERGY: The body's reaction to a substance causing unpleasant or annoying symptoms

BAKING PAPER: Silicone-coated paper for baking; available in supermarkets

BATTER: Runny mixture of flour and liquid

BLEND: Mix the ingredients together

CRUST: Hard outside layer of bread

DOUGH: Firm mixture of flour and other ingredients

FOLD: Lightly combine a dry product into a moist mixture using a folding motion

GLAZE: Thin coating of egg, syrup or aspic used to coat bread or pastry

GLUTEN: Protein formed in wheat, oats, barley, rye, triticale and spelt

GREASE: Coat with soft margarine or other grease to prevent food sticking

INTOLERANCE: The body's inability to digest or cope with a food or other product

GEL: Form a jelly. Let stand until mixture thickens

KNEAD: Working dough to add air by turning and rolling

KNOCK BACK: Releasing the gas formed by the yeast by stirring the batter. This refines the texture of the loaf by breaking the bubbles formed by the yeast

LINSEEDS: Long brown seeds with a nutty flavour available in health food shops

MELT: Place food in a saucepan or microwave and heat gently until it becomes a liquid

MIX: To evenly combine ingredients

OIL: In my recipes I use Italian olive oil; other vegetable oils can be used

PATE: Paste of meat or spread

PUFFY: Slightly inflated appearance

RISE/RAISE: Set aside for a period of time to allow leavening ingredient to expand

SET ASIDE: Leave the mixture to stand for a period of time

SIFT: Pass through a fine wire or plastic mesh to refine products

SOFTEN: With gelatine: sprinkle over cold water and leave to stand for a few minutes

SPRINKLE: Scatter or drop small particles on top

THICKEN: Produce a creamy product from a thin liquid by adding starch or a sauce block

WHIP: Rapidly mix adding air, using wire or electric beater

WHISK: Mix to add air to batter using a wire egg whisk or rotary beater

ZEST: Thin yellow layer of citrus skin

CONVERSION TABLE

APPROXIMATE QUANTITIES ROUNDED TO USABLE UNITS

Metric cup measures are available in most countries; it is advisable to use them instead of guessing or using a kitchen cup. The conversion quantities given are approximate, rounded to the most practical unit; they are not as accurate as the metric measurements. My recipes use the Australian tablespoon that is 20g. Beware that American tablespoons measure 15g, so an additional level teaspoon of the ingredient must be used to achieve the same result.

LIQUIDS

1 metric cup = 250mL
$\frac{1}{2}$ metric cup = 125mL
$\frac{1}{3}$ metric cup = 80mL
$\frac{1}{4}$ metric cup = 65mL

DRY INGREDIENTS

50g = approx. 2oz
100g = approx. 4oz
250g = approx. 8.5oz
450g = approx. 16 oz

SPOONS

1 teaspoon = 5g
1 tablespoon = 20g

OVEN TEMPERATURE

140°C / 275°F / gas mark 1
160°C / 325°F / gas mark 3
180°C / 350°F / gas mark 4
200°C / 400°F / gas mark 6
240°C / 475°F / gas mark 9

INDEX